Brewery Operations Volume 8

1991 Transcripts from the
National Microbrewers Conference

Edited by Virginia Thomas

Brewers Publications
Boulder, Colorado USA

Brewing Under Adversity
Brewery Operations Vol. 8
Edited by Virginia Thomas
Copyright ©1992 Association of Brewers

ISBN 0-937381-29-2
Printed in the United States of America

Published by Brewers Publications
a division of the Association of Brewers
P.O. Box 1679, Boulder, Colorado 80306-1679 USA
Tel. (303) 447-0816, FAX (303) 447-2825

Direct all inquiries/orders to the above address.

All rights reserved. Except for use in a review,
no portion of this book may be reproduced in any form
without the express written permission of the publisher.

Neither the authors, editor nor the publisher assumes
any responsibility for the use or misuse of
information contained in this book.

Cover design by David Bjorkman

Photographs by David Bjorkman-National News Service

Table of Contents

1991 NATIONAL MICROBREWERS CONFERENCE

Acknowledgments.....ix

Foreword.....xi

1. Brewing Under Adversity....1
    Michael Lewis, Ph.D.

2. Sources of Power in the Brewhouse.....11
    Eric Warner

3. Tapping into History with a Renovated Brewpub.....25
    John Hickenlooper

4. Angles and Vultures: The Search for Financing.....37
    Stephen Dinehart III

5. Assuring the Best Beer.....47
    Richard Rench, Ph.D.

6. Insurance for Microbreweries.....67
   Peter Whalen

7. ATF and the Label-Approval Process.....75
   Jerry Bowerman

8. Distributing Microbrewed Beers.....87
   Thomas Potter

9. Brewpub Design Efficiency.....109
   Steve Fried

10. Industry Overview.....119
    David Edgar

11. Packaging for the Environment.....139
    Beth Michelman Gross

12. Multi-Unit Operations.....145
    Dean Biersch

13. The Marketing of Draft vs. Bottled Beer.....161
    Peter McAuslan

14. The Business of Brewing.....173
    Jim Koch and Paul Shipman

15. Strategic Market Planning.....187
    Daniel Bradford

16. Achieving Stability Using Membrane Filtration.....201
    Peter Meier

17. Bioremediation: Nature's Way of Treating Wastewater.....217
    Sean Duddy

18. Industry Under Attack.....223
    Jeffrey G. Becker

19. Current Brewing Issues.....231
    W. Andrew Patton

Acknowledgments

THOSE WHO ASSISTED FINANCIALLY IN THIS BOOK

A special thanks to the following companies:

Adolph Coors Brewing Company, *Golden, Colorado*

Anheuser-Busch, Inc., *St. Louis, Missouri*

Boston Beer Company, *Boston, Massachusetts*

Briess Malting Company, *New York, New York*

Great Western Malting Company, *Vancouver, Washington*

Hopunion USA., Inc., *Yakima, Washington*

Hudepohl-Schoenling Brewing Company, *Cincinnati, Ohio*

Miller Brewing Company, *Milwaukee, Wisconsin*

Morris Hanbury, USA, Inc., *Yakima, Washington*

Redhook Ale Brewery, Inc., *Seattle, Washington*

Sierra Nevada Brewing Company, *Chico, California*

United Canadian Malt, Ltd., *Peterborough, Ontario, Canada*

Foreword

INTRODUCTION TO BREWING UNDER ADVERSITY

*Virginia Thomas,
Institute for Brewing Studies*

In the early 1980s, the men who opened the first microbreweries and brewpubs had to invent the "wheel" on which the movement would roll forward. They moved ahead in an environment characterized by a dearth of small-scale brewing equipment; no financial history to show lenders; no ready market of customers; prohibitive legislation; and a lack of information on the process of brewing good, saleable beer in batches larger than homebrew but smaller than a few hundred thousand barrels. In short, industry pioneers in North America faced a climate in which there was no working, domestic model where they could learn how to operate their microbreweries and brewpubs and market their beer. As they grew their business, they faced the major adversity of inexperience.

They did have one advantage, however, that served them: they formed relationships with their peers in which they could share their experiences and enthusiasm. They opened their doors to newcomers into the industry, and as more people opened and operated small breweries nationwide, they traveled to conferences where they related their experiences in problem solving. Today, the microbrewing industry has grown to more than 350 breweries that

have all benefitted from brewers' willingness to get together and share information.

The nineteen chapters in this book were originally presented at the 1991 National Microbrewers Conference and Trade Show in Buffalo, New York, in September 1991. The topics address the diverse concerns of brewers: brewing high-quality beer under adversity, neoprohibition vs. responsible beer consumption, growing a brand, selling through self-distribution, and opening markets.

As the editor of these chapters, I have enjoyed working on such a worthwhile project, one that has such potential to enhance the industry through providing information. My thanks to the authors and to David Bjorkman of National News Service, whose superb photographs allow you to better know the authors.

To the reader, I wish you a valuable and enjoyable read. I hope you profit from it.

*Virginia Thomas has been the editor-in-chief of **The New Brewer** since it began in 1983. As a founding member of the staff of the Institute for Brewing Studies, she has watched the microbrewing industry almost from its inception. She is a writer and journalist whose work on terrorism and Latin American conflicts has appeared in numerous national and foreign magazines.*

Chapter 1.

BREWING UNDER ADVERSITY

Michael J. Lewis, Ph.D., University of California-Davis

The function of a keynote address is to review the theme of the conference and to put it in perspective. To be frank, that sounds simple enough, but other challenges arise: to do the job succinctly but with crystal clarity; to do it wisely but with compelling humor; to be complete without encroaching on the presentations of others; to have penetrating insight without anticipating other's ideas, and to do this all in exactly the required time, without controversy and without offending the organizers, exhibitors and sponsors of the events. That's a challenge.

The theme "Brewing Under Adversity" is a compelling one of interest to all brewers, though depending on where they stand in the hierarchy of corporate size and influence, brewers might order adversities differently. Any brewer's list of adversities could include new and different labeling requirements; new and higher taxes; new restrictions on advertising; the stormy economic climate and the egregious cost of everything worth having; alcohol and society and health; production and manufacturing challenges of all sorts; safety issues and effluent disposal; and the rising tide of prohibitionism. The list could be made a good deal longer, but I find

no adversities that fall outside three main rubrics — economics or the Adversity of Profit, society or the Adversity of Prohibition, and technical or the Adversity of Ignorance.

I was about to embark on a simple exposition of these adversities when three complications struck me at about the same time: adversity is not contemporary; these adversities are not necessarily all bad all of the time; and different breweries have different concerns.

The climate for brewing has not suddenly or even recently gone from sunny to cloudy to stormy. Brewers have always brewed under adversity, and those adversities have always been partly economic, partly prohibitionary, and partly technical, though the importance of one aspect or another has dominated at different times in brewing history. Nevertheless, this conference theme could have been sounded at any time during the 5,000-year recorded history of brewing. Though the quality of the adversities pressed upon brewers may have changed over the centuries (but not by much!), brewers have always managed the adversities and problems thrust upon them by their profession and trade. Adversity is part and parcel of brewing, and it always has been. In fact, the adversities we suffer, more or less with dignity, I hope, link us to our brewing antecedents as much as anything else we do as craft brewers.

Nor indeed are these adversities necessarily all bad all of the time. A slight economic chill may have advantages; the Adversity of Profit encourages and rewards sound business practices and helps weed out the unhealthful so that the stronger may thrive. A little bit of the Adversity of Prohibition in the air may be as bracing as the first snowflake of Fall; it reminds us of the very real social responsibilities that go with our right to brew beer and sell it. And even a measure of the Adversity of Ignorance, in a curious way, helps conserve the mystery and magic of what we do in the brewery to produce beer — that magic potion — and how we achieve the extraordinary range of beers available in today's marketplace.

Not all brewers are affected to the same degree by the same adversity. Thus, any restriction on advertising, for example, is a grave adversity for major brewers who distinguish their products substantially by advertising with advertising budgets of many millions. (At one of our sensory courses, thirty microbrewers as a group could not distinguish by flavor Coors from Budweiser at a statistically significant level; of course, this may say as much about the tasters as the products!) The local microbrewery relying on word-of-mouth promotion and an advertising budget of fifty bucks is unlikely to be as concerned about adversity in advertising. Yet, because he suffers the penalties of small scale, he may be aghast at the cost of raw materials and packaging supplies, the egregious price of well-designed and well-built equipment, and the absence of necessary Quality Assurance technology that is affordable.

Let me discuss now the three rubrics of adversity I identified earlier.

The Adversity of Profit. Of course, profit itself is not the adversity; the adversity is the continuing need to make a profit. Brewing (except homebrewing) is not a hobby or sport but a serious and expensive business. In the face of hard economic reality, unplanned, ill-conceived and unmanaged operations are doomed to fail; fortunately, they usually fail quickly. Business acumen is not unique to brewing, and I have no special expertise in it, but I do recommend your close attention to those presentations at this conference that are devoted to management.

The Adversity of Prohibition. Prohibition or neoprohibition (probably so called to make it sound contemporary or more threatening, or to accentuate its changing face) arose as a human emotion shortly after the first tipsy Teamster fell off his camel 3,000 years before Christ, and it has ebbed and flowed ever since. I don't mind teetotalers any more than I mind vegetarians or those who run marathons. Individuals are entitled to drink and eat and do what they choose and to express their opinion about their preference. But teetotalers are not necessarily prohibitionists.

I applaud those who are concerned about problems of alcohol abuse in our society and work toward their solution. Our industry has joined with such groups because no sane person or entity can argue for drinking and driving (for example), and if alcohol causes birth defects, the public has a right to be warned about that. These folks are not necessarily prohibitionists, either. (There is not a prohibitionist under every bush.) There are issues about alcohol in our society that the alcohol beverage industry needs to take seriously, and I think for the most part does.

The neo-prohibitionist, however, seizes upon legitimate social concerns to create a climate in which the ultimate prohibitionist agenda (ban) is advanced. Such people wish to dictate to me my habits of consumption, and I object very strongly to that. If prohibitionists can create a climate in which abuse of our product is seen to be the behavioral norm (and the microbrewing and homebrewing industry has some maturing to do in this regard); or a climate in which the poisonous/unhealthful aspects of moderate consumption are promoted at the expense of the refreshing/beneficial aspects ("alcohol and other drugs"); if prohibitionists can project the image of the young, poor, impressionable, and witless as dupes of corporate greed who are entrapped by irresponsible advertising; then prohibitionists can create the contemporary antialcohol climate in which our current adversities are exacerbated — not merely taxation but "sin taxes," not responsible advertising but censorship, not moderate consumption but "restriction of supply."

Prohibition hinges primarily on public perception. Microbrewers, along with the major brewers, are part of the same public perception of the beer industry and microbrewers must play a role in creating the image that brewers and breweries are good corporate citizens. Much of the microbrewing industry has grown up from the homebrewing industry and retains strong traces of attitudes towards beer brewing and consumption that reflect the lais'sez faire approach of brewing for personal consumption. The microbrewing industry has to thoughtfully take its place with the majors in presenting a sober face to the public, dull as that may seem. All brewers are wise to remember there is nothing so intolerable as a drunken brewer, and that a life spent in the alcohol beverage industry is one of moderation and sobriety.

The Adversity of Ignorance. For a moment, please sympathize with Ptolemy the Baker who invented beer in the year 3000 BC. He arrives home with a sad face. His wife Cleopatra greets him in an upbeat way, "Hi, Ptol. What's up?"

Miserably he tells her that the second batch of the new product he developed last week to use up unsold bread (and which his customers were calling the best thing since the loaf) turned out really badly. "You know that new product — drinkable bread? Okay, so we have to think of a better name for it, well, the second batch stinks."

Cleo asked the hard question, "Did you make it the same way as the first time?"

The word consistency, incidentally, is Latin and hadn't been invented yet.

"Of course Cleo! I used an incantation from the Rameses Liturgy at the soak, three vestal virgins stood guard during foaming-up, and I did the Lughnasad dance we learned from that Celtic trader while potting the slop. Okay, we need a new term for that, too."

Cleo knew a good thing when she saw it. "Wow!" she said, "Nothing wrong with those procedures!"

We have brewers today who repeat incantations to which they

Pre-Conference Tour participants are treated to a fine Arkell Best Bitter while visiting the Wellington County Brewery in Guelph, Ontario.

ascribe their success, and one could argue that modern advertising slogans are the direct descendant of Ptolemy's prayers — and have just as much to do with good beer. But the point I want to make is that Ptolemy's adversity was the greatest one of all—the Adversity of Ignorance.

Brewers remained scientifically ignorant for the next 4,900 years after Ptolemy — practical microbiology and biochemistry are barely a century or so old. We, as modern brewers, do not suffer from the Adversity of Ignorance, at least, not in the same way or to the same extent as Ptolemy and the 4,900 years'-worth of brewers who followed him. To tell the truth, we are not really ignorant at all as long as we stay within the normal realms of brewing experience; however, our lack of knowledge promptly emerges even in modern brewing practice when we stray from normal practice. To an extent, I am only now beginning to realize that microbrewing as it is practiced today is often a radical departure from normal procedures. But how did our antecedent brewers handle their adversity?

They learned to live with it, of course. Most particularly they developed their craft by accumulating knowledge based on empiricism and observation, and they banded together in guilds and professional societies to share their knowledge with each other and to protect their knowledge from the unsuited. We do the same today; we are doing the same here at this conference.

The point is that the most telling adversity—lack of knowledge (of amylase or yeast for goodness sake!)—was managed by brewers from whom we are directly descended. Are we unable to handle today's adversities? Professionalism and pride and perseverance sustained brewers through adversities in the past and remain our watchwords today.

Fortunately, the Adversity of Ignorance is one that can be fought without controversy and confrontation. Experience, training, education, and qualification are all positive words and the means by which ignorance is dispelled. But these are not the same thing: experience is the skill to do something; training is instruction in that skill; education is understanding the skill; and qualification is the means by which all three are measured and quantified. Education is the great accelerator of experience and training. Qualification is the coinage of education.

If there is the Adversity of Ignorance, there are organizations whose function is to help dispel it; this organization, the Institute for Brewing Studies, is one of them. One function of my program at the University of California, Davis, is to help in this task. Our program is the only program in the country leading to a formal qualification relevant to the field (B.S. Fermentation Science) and is a well-known qualification in the U.S. industry. Many UC-Davis graduates have established an extraordinary record of accomplishment and success in large and small breweries alike. Unfortunately, the degree program is inaccessible to many who would wish to take it. For this reason we run several short courses, as does the Siebel

& Sons Company (including its famous ten-week course) and others. But these short courses do not lead to formal qualifications of any kind.

We now seek to remedy that by putting in place a nine-month residential program at UC-Davis—the course work will also be available by correspondence (i.e., instruction by mail)—the function of which is to prepare candidates for the Associate Members Examination of the Institute of Brewing in London. This is an internationally recognized examination and qualification that has much to offer the American brewing industry in large and small companies alike and for individuals who would join the industry. The Institute strictly controls the examination, decides who may take it, and absolutely defines who passes and who does not. This guards the integrity of the qualification. The examination comprises three parts: two brewing papers and an engineering paper. The first class is gathering now, and the next will open in Fall 1992.

Let me draw my presentation to a close. Brewers today are no different from their antecedents in the profession; they do and will brew under adversity—whether those adversities be economic, social or technical. And, as brewers have always done, today's brewers will face those challenges and in overcoming them, prosper. Unlike so many modern industries, brewers can point with pride to the long history of their profession and draw special strength from their right and proper association with humankind from its earliest recorded history. I urge you to follow the footsteps of your antecedents—join your guilds and support them, persevere, take pride in the profession and act accordingly, and guard the quality of the product.

Michael J. Lewis, Ph.D., is Professor of Brewing Science in the Department of Food Science and Technology at the University of California-Davis, California. He has served on the Board of Gov-

ernors of the Master Brewers Association of America and is a member of the American Society of Brewing Chemists and the Institute of Brewing. He is the author of numerous papers on brewing and a teacher and adviser to dozens of brewers.

For information about the program leading to examination by the Institute of Brewing in London, call the UC-Davis Extension at (916) 757-8899.

Chapter 2.

SOURCES OF POWER IN THE BREWHOUSE

*Eric Warner,
Boulder, Colorado*

At least 40 percent of the total primary energy used in a brewery is consumed in the brewhouse, and for those breweries that don't bottle, this figure is significantly higher. The energy needed to power the brewhouse can range from 60,000 to 140,000 BTU (15 to 35 Mcal) per barrel of packaged beer. There was a time when primary sources of energy seemed to grow on trees, but the recent crisis in the Persian Gulf and the controversy over tapping the oil in the Arctic National Wildlife Refuge remind us not only of how dramatically fossil fuel prices can climb, but also of the burden the world's ecosystems must bear so we can use fossil fuels to energize our cars, planes and breweries.

Choosing the right source of power for a brewery is not only a quantitative question, but a qualitative one as well. Certain means of powering a brewhouse make sense in terms of cost accounting, but they may not add up when it comes to producing a particular style of beer. The modern brewer is faced with four options to power the brewhouse: electricity, direct firing of brewing vessels, steam, and hot water. In the following discussion, the practicality and effectiveness of each of these power sources for the brewhouse,

as well as the current state-of-the-art techniques for energy efficient brewing, will be investigated in order that the twenty-first century brewer can make the best possible beer with a minimal impact on the environment. In the second section of this discussion, the possible means for recovering the heat used in the brewhouse will be examined so that the primary energy input into the brewhouse can be as minimal as possible.

Direct Heating of Brewing Vessels

Electricity as a source of brewhouse power is fine for basement brewing but should not be implemented for microbrewing on a commercial level for two main reasons. Primarily, the electricity obtained from the local power company has been generated by the company, and all of the costs associated with providing the electricity must be absorbed by the consumer. In other words, it is cheaper to purchase natural gas from the local energy monopoly and use a burner to heat the brewing vessels than to purchase electricity from the power company. Another problem associated with the use of electricity as a source of brewhouse power is the caramelization of the wort that can take place as a result of the extremely high temperature at the heat transfer surface of the electric unit(s). This is particularly undesirable if pale or lager beers are being produced. The only possible advantage to using electricity as a source of brewhouse heat is the low investment necessary for such a system. This low capital expenditure however, will soon be overshadowed by the higher utility costs for operating such an inefficient system.

The direct firing of the brewing vessels represents the oldest method for wort boiling. There are many small European breweries that still use coal to heat the brewkettles, and I even know of one that uses wood. Today, oil and natural gas are the main choices for modern breweries that use direct kettle heating, and natural gas is the more popular choice because it is easier to use and burns cleaner. Oil is often the cheaper of the two, and therein lies its appeal.

The firing units usually function as two-step burners, and with larger brewkettles there may be several burners, thus allowing for more control in the heating process. The flame itself does not come into contact with the bottom of the brewhouse vessels, rather the flue gases rush past the exterior surface of the brewkettle. Temperatures on the flame side of the kettle may reach 1,000 degrees F (537 degrees C). Kettle shape is not as important with direct-flame systems as it is with indirectly heated systems, and kettle bottoms may be flat, concave or convex. In order that the desired boiling effect be achieved, the burners must be capable of producing 33,300 BTU of heat per barrel (30,000 kJ/hl) of cast out wort. In other terms, the burner must be capable of producing 280,000 BTU (65 kW) for a seven-barrel system. Degrees of efficiency as high as 70 percent can be reached with a direct-fired brew kettle, assuming the system is well insulated.

The primary advantage of direct-fired brewkettles for microbrewers is the reduced cost. A steam-powered brewhouse costs more because the kettles must be jacketed or fitted with steam pipes, a boiler must be purchased to produce the steam, water treatment must be undertaken for the boiler feed water, and some type of condensate diversion system must be implemented. The problem with direct-fired systems is that the brewer has less control over the wort boiling process. Particularly, the microbrewer has difficulty controlling the temperature of the kettle bottom if there is only one two-stage burner in use. The result can be higher than desired degrees of caramelization in the kettle wort. This is particularly problematic if light lagers are being brewed. For the brewery that is making darker, heavier beers, this is not such a problem, and direct-flame brewing systems are very common in small North American breweries.

Indirect Heating of Brewing Vessels

Steam has long been the choice of major breweries for a source of power in the brewhouse. Indeed, large breweries often have steam-generated power plants with which they power the entire brewery. Unfortunately, this is not an option for microbrewers because of cost. Many microbreweries, however, do use steam derived from boilers to power the brewing vessels. Although steam-powered brewhouses are more capital intensive than those powered by direct flame or electricity, using steam as a source of power in the brewhouse provides a number of advantages.

Many microbrewers use steam boilers that produce steam of 15 psi (1.1 bar) overpressure. If pressures higher than this are used, then the boiler may have to be ASME certified, thus raising the cost of the boiler. A very common steam pressure for many brewhouse operations is 43.5 psi (3 bar) overpressure. We will soon see why it is more advantageous to use steam of this pressure than steam of 15 psi (1.1 bar).

It is important that the feed water for the boilers be of the right quality, otherwise deposits may lower the efficiency of the boiler and/or result in corrosion. The quality of the feed water is dependent upon the type of boiler, and in general, the higher the operating pressure of the boiler, the greater the requirements of the water quality. The hardness of the feed water must be very low, less than 1 ppm, otherwise the efficiency of the boiler may be reduced by mineral deposits. It is also important that the oxygen and carbon dioxide contents of the feed water be low, otherwise corrosion may occur. The levels should be less than 20µg/l and 5mg/l, respectively. The pH of the feed water should be high, particularly if the water contains a lot of salts. The pH can be adjusted upward using sodium hydroxide. Iron levels in the water should be low, less than 30µg/l. It is also important to measure the silicic acid content of the boiler water, as higher than desired amounts can lead to the development of deposits in the boiler that are difficult to remove.

The design of brewing vessels powered by steam varies somewhat from the design of vessels that are directly fired. Whereas the bottom of a direct-fired brewkettle may be concave, kettles heated with steam often have a convex bottom. Brewkettles have been designed in all shapes over the years, and to go into detail here would go beyond the scope of the topic at hand, but what is important is how the steam jackets are integrated into the kettle. A brewkettle with an apparently logical design is useless if the steam jackets are not properly dimensioned and positioned. Conversely, brewkettles with odd shapes or designs can function well if the steam jackets are properly designed.

In designing the steam jackets/heat-transfer surfaces, it is important that the following objectives be met:

1. The heat transfer surface must be large enough to achieve the desired evaporation rate of the wort.

2. The temperature of the steam, or more correctly, the pressure of the steam, must be orchestrated with the size of the heat transfer surface so the first objective is met.

3. The placement of the steam jackets/heat-transfer surfaces must promote effective convection in that all wort particles contact the heat-transfer surface, thus precluding dead zones in the kettle.

Objectives one and two are by nature related, so they will be handled together. The flow of heat, Q, is defined as:

$$Q = (t_2 - t_1) * k * A,$$

where k is the heat transfer coefficient. k is a constant that incorporates many factors and differs from case to case. A is the area of the heat transfer surface. k assumes its largest value for condensing steam. In the case of water at or near the boiling point, k may only be 33 to 50 percent that of condensing steam. Solving for A, it is quickly evident that the heat transfer surface would have to be two or three times greater for water than for steam. Looking at the other variable in the equation, the difference in temperature, we also see that A can be reduced when delta *t* is greater. Assuming that the wort boiling is taking place at atmospheric pressure, this means that process steam of a higher pressure increases this variable. Steam at 1 bar has a temperature of 212 degrees F (100 degrees C), and steam at 3 bar a temperature of 273 degrees F (134 degrees C). Since *t*1 is at 212 degrees F (100 degrees C), we can see that this variable is increased when the steam is of a higher pressure.

To better understand how steam jackets need to be dimensioned, let's look at the following examples:

Volume of wort at boil begin:	20 hl
Rate of evaporation:	8 %/ hr
Density of water at 212° F (100° C):	0.96 kg/l
Steam pressure:	3 bar
Corresponding Temperature:	273° F (134° C)
k value for this scenario:	2000 W/m2 * °K
Enthalpy (h) of steam at 1 bar:	2257 kJ/kg

Now, we know that the flow of energy going into the system equals the flow exiting the system once the wort is boiling. To calculate the flow of energy going into the system, and subsequently the necessary heat transfer surface area, we simply calculate the energy leaving the system using the information we have for the water vapor leaving the brewkettle:

$$Q_{in} = Q_{out}$$
$$Q_{out} = V_{vapor} * D_{vapor} * h_{vapor}$$
$$Q_{out} = 160 \text{ l/hr} * 0.96 \text{ kg/l} * 2257 \text{ kJ/kg}$$
$$Q_{out} = 346{,}675 \text{ kJ/hr} = Q_{in}$$
$$Q_{in} = (t2-t1) * k * A$$

Solving for the area 'A':

$$A = Q_{in} / (t2-t1) * k$$
$$A = \frac{346{,}675 \text{ kJ/hr}}{34^\circ \text{ K} \times 2 \text{ kW/m2*K} \times 3600 \text{ kJ/kW*h}}$$
$$A = 1.4 \text{ m2} = 15 \text{ ft2}$$

If the pressure of the steam were half of what it is in this example, its temperature would be only 231 degrees F (111 degrees C), and the surface area for heat transfer would have to be tripled. Thus, it is easy to see that the pressure of the process steam greatly influences the necessary area of the heat-transfer surface in the steam-powered brewkettle.

The third criterion for the proper dimensioning of a steam-powered brewkettle is the placement of the steam jackets themselves in the brewkettle. Even if the size of the jackets has been properly calculated for the given pressure of the steam, placing the jackets incorrectly in the kettle can result in a vigorous boil, but one that may give rise to dead zones in the wort. Mounting half of the necessary jacket area on the bottom of the kettle, and the other half on the side, works well with flat brewkettles, but can lead to dead zones in kettles with a round bottom. A popular choice among many brewhouse engineers is to use two different pressures of steam in the two zones of the jacketing. If both zones of the jacketing are on the bottom of the kettle, then the inner zone is fed with steam of higher pressure, and the outer zone with lower-pressure steam. This helps to circulate the wort from the middle to the side of the kettle and results in a thorough mixing of the wort during boiling.

Many brewkettles are fitted with internal wort boilers, and this is a commonly found construction in both older and newer breweries. The more primitive construction entails having a steampipe ring at the bottom of the kettle. Modern constructions have a bundle of open-ended pipes held together in a giant cylinder, which is placed in the middle of the kettle. The wort flows through the pipes, and the steam circulates around them, forcing the wort in an upward direction.

Whichever type of boiler or jacketing a brewery may use, it is important that the condensate diversion be effective in order that the heat transfer be maximized. Larger breweries may opt for a closed condensate diversion system so the greatest amount of the steam's energy can be retained. This system, in which the condensate is kept at a pressure equal to that of the steam in the jacket or boiler, is far more energy efficient than open condensate diversion systems. Open condensation at atmospheric pressure is more wasteful, simply because the post evaporation of the condensate at atmospheric pressure brings it down to a lower energy niveau.

Why is steam the first choice as a source of heat for the brewhouse in breweries worldwide? First, it is much easier to regulate the process of wort boiling using steam instead of electricity or a direct flame. Monitoring the temperature of the process steam is made easy simply by knowing the pressure of the steam. Also, using steam results in a gentler boiling of the wort because the temperature of the condensing steam at the heat transfer surface is much less than in direct fired systems. Because of this, there is less wort caramelization when steam is used, and thus steam is the only choice for making smooth, pale lagers. Another big advantage of a steam-powered brewery is that the steam from the boiler can be used in other areas of the brewery for sterilization and heating.

The primary disadvantage of using steam to power a microbrewery is the increased capital expenditure. For smaller breweries in particular, the costs of a boiler, feed water preparation, steam lines and condensate diversion may be too high to warrant implementation. Hidden costs in terms of increased labor costs for water preparation and boiler maintenance/supervision must also be accounted for.

At this point, the use of hot water to power brewhouse vessels should be mentioned briefly. The appeal of using hot water for brewhouse power lies quite simply in the fact that the entire problem of condensate diversion found in steam-powered breweries is avoided, and thus heat losses encountered with condensate diversion are non-existent. The drawback to using hot water as a power source in the brewhouse is its increased capital expenditure. Pipelines and armatures must be designed more strongly, the heat transfer surfaces must be larger, and costly hot water pumps must be implemented. Although some breweries do use hot water as a source of brewhouse heat, the increased installation costs make this option unattractive for many microbreweries.

Heat Recovery Options in the Brewhouse

I would like to examine the possibilities for heat recovery in the brewhouse, or in simpler terms how the least amount of primary energy can be used to power the brewhouse. These issues are of less concern to the pubbrewer, but if energy prices climb to unprecedented levels, brewers both large and small will be forced to minimize energy expenses.

There is one way in which every brewer can recover a large amount of heat from the cast out wort, and that is by using the plate heat exchanger. It is essential that the plate heat exchanger be properly designed to recover the greatest amount of heat from the wort. The most efficient heat exchangers are divided into pre- and post-cooling zones. In the first zone, brewing water is used, and in the post-cooling zone, a coolant such as glycol or chilled water cools the wort to the desired pitching temperature.

The plate heat exchanger should meet the following criteria so the heat recovery from the cast out wort is maximized:

1. The ratio of water used in the pre-cooling zone of the heat exchanger to the quantity of cast out wort should be 1 to 1.1:1. If more water than this is used, two things occur. First, the temperature of the wort as it leaves the pre-cooling zone is higher than if less water is used to cool the wort in the same period of time. Second, the temperature of the water, which will be used for the next brew, will be considerably less than the water coming from a properly dimensioned heat exchanger.

Worse, the brewer using an improperly designed heat exchanger has to pay not just once, but twice, or even three times for this engineering flaw:

• The brewing water recovered from the wort cooling process should be at or above sparge temperature, at approximately 176 degrees F (80 degrees C). Water obtained from an ill-designed heat exchanger is less than this, so energy has to be expended to heat the sparge water to the proper temperature.

• Because the temperature of the wort leaving the pre-cooling zone of the improperly designed heat exchanger is greater than that of the wort from the properly designed heat exchanger, more heat must be exchanged in the post-cooling zone, thus requiring the coolant pump and the compressor to work harder than they should. The result is higher than necessary electricity bills. The effects of this can be particularly dramatic for larger breweries making classically fermented lagers, as these worts need to be cooled to low pitching temperatures.

• Finally, the increased quantity of water used in the pre-cooling zone of the plate heat exchanger often results in increased effluent loads. This is an unnecessary waste that can, depending on the size of the brewery, effect higher sewage tariffs.

2. The difference in temperature between the wort coming out

of the pre-cooling zone and the water going into it should not exceed 5.5 degrees F (3 degrees C). This serves as a good barometer for measuring the efficiency of the precooling zone.

3. For qualitative reasons, the wort should be cooled in less than one hour to avoid an unwanted deepening of color and to prevent the development of DMS in the wort.

Another means of recovering heat from the wort boiling process is the use of kettle vapor condensers. Heat that otherwise escapes the brewery can be recovered using such vapor condensers. The vapors escaping from the surface of the boiling wort are pressed into a heat exchanger—a plate heat exchanger, for example —using a fan. The system has to be airtight for the efficiency of the system to be high. When the system is properly designed, approximately 4.5 to 5.4 barrels (5.5 to 6.5 hl) of water can be heated from 54 to176 degrees F (12 to 80 degrees C) per hectoliter of vapor. Although this isn't enough water to cover the warm brewing water needs of a brewery (and the warm brewing water is usually obtained from the wort cooling process), this warm water can be used in other parts of the brewery or brewpub for cleaning or heating. Simple kettle vapor condensers can be purchased for as little as $3,000 to $5,000, a sum that may be a bit high for brewpub operators, but well within reason for a good-sized microbrewery.

One of the simplest tricks to reduce brewhouse energy input is to boil the wort for less time and/or under pressure. While this procedure may reduce energy consumption in the brewhouse, it may also be associated with qualitative drawbacks. Driving off DMS-P is not the only issue to be considered here; rather, it is essential that other volatile substances that negatively affect the flavor of the finished beer also be driven off. Wort boiling times at atmospheric pressure and at 212 degrees F (100 degrees C) should not be less than 80 minutes. If low pressure boiling is considered, then it is important that the following process criteria be met:

- The wort boiling temperature should not exceed 220 degrees F (105 degrees C), otherwise the resulting beers will have a boiled wort taste, and protein precipitation could be greater than desired, resulting in foam stability problems.
- The total evaporation should be at least 8 percent.
- The wort should be boiled at atmospheric pressure for up to 15 minutes before and after it is boiled under pressure to drive off unwanted volatile substances and to achieve 8 percent total evaporation.

Although these methods for wort boiling are energy saving, caution must be taken if they are employed since the beers from underboiled or pressure-boiled worts may have off-aromas.

One of the more elegant wort-boiling systems is the external wort boiler coupled with a vapor compressor. The boiler itself is actually a multi-tube or plate heat exchanger through which steam and the wort pass in opposing directions. It is mounted outside the wort kettle, which usually doubles as a pre-run and whirlpool vessel. The wort is circulated through the external boiler and then pumped back into the combi-vessel. Tremendous energy savings are realized if the system uses a vapor compressor to return the steam rising from the surface of the wort to a higher energy level. This compressed steam is returned to the boiler where it is used to boil the wort in conjunction with steam from the main brewery steam boiler.

It is important that the design of the kettle be such that the wort is thoroughly and evenly distributed throughout the vessel. Dead zones in an external wort boiling system can be extremely detrimental to the quality of the beer since the particles in these zones never come in contact with the heating surface. The beauty of a kettle used with an external wort boiler is that the bottom of the kettle can be flat and thus function perfectly as a whirlpool. Conventionally heated kettles designed in this way do not produce a rolling boil that evenly distributes the wort particles throughout the liquid, and kettles with rounded bottoms do not function as a whirlpool as well as flat-bottom vessels do.

To realize the greatest energy savings, the vapor compression system should be free of air. After the wort has been heated, and the system is free of air, the vapors are compressed using a diesel, gas or electric motor. Depending on the efficiency of the system, the heat needed to boil the wort can be reduced by more than 50 percent. Also, the beers produced from such systems are totally devoid of off-aromas or off-flavors that may be present in beers brewed using pressure boiling. Unfortunately, the capital expenditure is greater for this system, so it is amortizable only for regional or larger microbreweries.

Eric Warner is president of Blue River Brewing Consultants, in Lafayette, Colorado, advising breweries on equipment and brewing processes. He holds a brewing diploma from Weihenstephan in Munich. He has been published in **The New Brewer.**

Chapter 3.

TAPPING INTO HISTORY WITH A RENOVATED BREWPUB

John Hickenlooper, Wynkoop Brewing Co.

Brewpubs became one of the success stories of the Eighties, and appear to be mushrooming into the Nineties. From coast to coast, brewpubs are generating the high yields associated with traditional restaurant investments, but at significantly reduced risk. A rule of thumb in the restaurant business is that eight out of ten will fail within the first two years. Brewpubs are so far succeeding at an inverse rate, with only two failing out of ten.

At the same time, brewpubs are uniquely suited to historic locations. The brewpub renaissance harkens back to the late nineteenth century, when there were more than 2,000 breweries in the United States, over ninety in Philadelphia alone. Many of these were neighborhood taverns with their own small breweries, what we now call brewpubs. This historic context, along with the strong earnings capability, allows potential brewpub entrepreneurs the rare opportunity to make money and do "good works" at the same time.

The U.S. as a country is still in its infancy compared to European counterparts, and this immaturity is demonstrated by its relative indifference to its architectural heritage. In Europe it is

almost impossible to tear down a building over a century old, no matter its condition. In this country landmarks are being razed in every city on a regular basis. Too often, the ruthless developer claims there is no economically viable alternative, no use that can generate the cash-flow necessary to justify the hundreds of thousands of dollars needed for renovation. The historic preservation movement, still in its infancy as well, desperately needs models that show that preservation and renovation can make economic sense. Enter brewpubs.

Brewpubs make economic sense. At least in these early stages of the brewpub revolution, the risk is low, and the return upon the success of the venture more than compensates the entrepreneur for the additional costs resulting from historic renovation. Every city in this country with a population greater than 100,000 could save at least one historic structure through judicious siting of a brewpub.

If you are planning a brewpub anyway, choosing an historic location not only reduces the risk of failure, but also helps increase your profit once you succeed. Brewpubs afford us the rare opportunity wherein doing good is good business.

An historic site helps contribute to a number of aspects of a brewpub's success, including ambience, marketing, financing and the bottom line. Its relative value will differ with each project, but the cumulative effect is usually greater than the simple sum of the individual parts. Synergy Ale.

I have helped design two brewpubs within historic structures in the past three years, in Denver and Fort Collins, Colorado. Both have met with great success. I am presently raising money for three more "historic" brewpubs, in Colorado Springs; Lincoln, Nebraska; and Rapid City, South Dakota. I'd like to use these projects to illustrate some of the practical (and not so practical) benefits of historic sites.

Let me add before beginning that a wonderful old building is not the most important ingredient in a successful brewpub. The most important factor is the beer. Wynkoop Brewing Company in Denver is successful because we have some of the best beer in the world. My brewing partner, Russell Schehrer, would be quick to remind me that old bricks have little affect on beer quality. Not that I don't occasionally wonder if the same beer doesn't taste a little better in a landmark building.

Ambience

Ambience, while not fermented, plays a critical part in a brewpub's success. It provides the context for the transcendental experience the public will enjoy at your bar. It is the atmosphere, the sense of place, that is so important in any restaurant.

The ambience of an historic building provides a natural environment for brewpubs. In most cases, brewpubs have higher ceilings and more graceful proportions than the modern budget-driven boxes of cinder block. If you are lucky, you can find a wealth of architectural detail still intact. At the Wynkoop, my partner, Jerry Williams, spent 150 hours restoring the original tin ceiling and cornice (see photo). We were lucky to have large arched windows and golden oak trim to contrast the maple floors. In a newer building such features would cost tens of thousands of dollars. At Wynkoop, a little spit, a little polish, and we had instant ambience. And even if you were to spend the money to put such features in a newer building, it could easily seem false and pretentious. As it would be. A brewpub should be grounded within its community, and not solely based on a trendy, upscale clientele that will move on in a few years as the next fad arrives. Just my personal opinion, but maybe worth considering.

An historic building allows a creative designer numerous opportunities to make bold statements, emphasizing visually the connection between the freshness of the beer and the casual

At Wynkoop, partner Jerry Williams spent 150 hours restoring the original tin ceiling and cornice.

elegance in which it is served. Antique back-bars, lighting fixtures, and traditional glassware are obvious examples.

Many historic buildings are located in historic neighborhoods, where the other old buildings create a context of their own. People go out not just to eat, but to get away from the sameness of their everyday life. They want to escape to a different place, where they will think different thoughts. Historic districts are perfect for this. Often such historic districts will attract a variety of restaurants and clubs, growing into entertainment districts.

Some cities have already redeveloped their historic neighborhoods and successfully promote them as such. The French Quarter in New Orleans and the Haymarket in Boston come immediately to mind. They are alive both day and night with people. But these are exceptions. Many cities are only just beginning to appreciate the value of long-ignored old neighborhoods and are unsure how to promote them. But the long-term success of rejuvenated historic districts, in this country and especially in Europe, clearly indicates that this will be a trend of the future.

Financing

For most incipient brewpub entrepreneurs, raising initial capital is the single greatest obstacle in getting open. Assuming the other ducks are in a row, having an historic location can greatly facilitate acquisition of capital.

I have no scientific data, but my impression is that preservation groups and history-focused community organizations are generally dominated by pillars of the community. Some would welcome the opportunity to help finance restoration projects, but have seldom been shown a deal that offers a feasible return on their investment.

Even for investors not infatuated with local heritage, locating a brewpub in a landmark lends the project credibility. It provides an aura of stability and security. Old photographs and architectural perspectives help a business plan stand out from the crowd—an asset since there are a lot of people out there competing for scant investment dollars.

Then there are tax credits. One of the last remaining federal tax credits is for renovating buildings listed on the National Register of Historic Places. If a project includes a little bit of leverage, say a bank loan and maybe leases on some of the equipment, investors could be guaranteed as much as a 20 percent return in the first year from tax savings alone. In the slow and sober nineties, these are impressive numbers.

Historic buildings are often a bit off the mainstream, which allows for the negotiation of lower rents. Wynkoop leased 12,000 square feet at a cost of only $1,000 per month for the first three years. This improves cash flow projections, enhancing the attraction of a brewpub investment. The out-of-the-way location can also be an advantage, especially if the building is located in an historic district. People perceive it as an attractive destination. The buildings are built at a human scale, which is more inviting, and less intimidating. There is the mystery and romance of the past, close at hand. As a result of a combination of factors, Wynkoop has averaged some 5,000 customers per week during the past year.

Marketing

Marketing is always a struggle between vision and budget. A new brewpub can afford only a fraction of the advertising it needs. Luckily newspapers still don't charge fees for writing features about brewpubs. Most historical societies are anchored by a few powerful media types, often senior editors at one of the local papers. While they might not write a story themselves, they easily can use their influence to get a story written.

Many of the beat and feature writers at newspapers have an equally strong feeling for history. I am uncertain why this is so. Perhaps reporters spend so much time uncovering facts and presenting them clearly that they develop an unusual fascination with history. The fact that most reporters, especially the seasoned vets, are avowed beer-hounds only amplifies the natural attraction. And any good reporter will tell you that many of their best tips and story ideas come at the end of a bar. Putting a brewpub in a building with a story behind it is like putting a jacuzzi in an oasis.

The influence of historic newsletters should not be underestimated. The Historic Denver News ran a full-page story on Wynkoop the month before opening. Although its circulation is less than 10,000, it includes many of the most influential members of the community. These people are opinion-makers, and they are pre-disposed to favor a brewpub located in an historic building. They'll talk about it far and wide.

A landmark building also offers endless graphic possibilities. Drawings or photographs of the building can be used for the logo and/or menus. Often, old buildings are connected in history with colorful personages who can be used in the restaurant menus and advertising to great effect. Coopersmith in Fort Collins distributes a flyer that features a drawing of the building and an explanation of the evolution of tenants leading up to the present-day brewpub.

Wynkoop Brewing Company is located on Wynkoop Street, and we regularly play up the connection with our namesake, Major Edward W. Wynkoop. Although a founder, first sheriff, and leading citizen of Denver, his conversion to the defense of the Indian way of life turned him into one of the territory's most hated individuals. We use his unsung role in the state's history on menus, flyers, and in a variety of advertising media.

Finally, old buildings are known for the complications and headaches involved in their renovation. This allows the clever entrepreneur an immediate opportunity to play the role of underdog. The anguish and catastrophes make good fodder for anecdotes on opening day, presenting the brewpub in a deservedly sympathetic light. The very process of dealing with the inevitable disasters, and of winning approvals from the various design and historic review boards, creates a network of allies. This is indeed the essence of marketing.

The Bottom Line

For many, perhaps the most compelling reasons for choosing an historic location over a more generic solution are the direct benefits to overall profitability. Foremost among these benefits are the federal (and in some cases state and city) tax credits available for historic renovation.

Keep in mind I am talking about a tax credit, not a simple deduction. A $25,000 credit is not deducted from your stated income, it is deducted from the final amount you owe. It is cash in your pocket. The Historic Investment Tax Credit (HITC) is one of the very few generally available federal tax credits remaining from the wide swathe of Reagan's tax "reform." Even so, it is not being widely taken advantage of because of the difficulty in finding good businesses that can support an expensive rehabilitation project. Other than brewpubs.

To qualify for the HITC, your building must be either on the National Register of Historic Places or a contributing building to a Historic District that is on the National Register. If your building is not so listed, in many cases it is no big deal to get it onto the register, assuming it has some history and architectural chutzpuh. Check with your local or state historical society, and in most cases, people there will go out of their way to walk you through the process.

Once it is on the Register, you are eligible for a 20 percent tax credit for all the money spent on the renovation, as long as this sum exceeds the purchase price of the space. This includes building permits, architect's fees, bathroom fixtures, and pretty much anything that is to remain a permanent part of the building. Unfortunately, this does not include kitchen or brewery equipment, tables, chairs, or other movable fixtures. The tax credit can be "carried forward" to be applied against future year's income if your income (or the brewpub's) isn't sufficient to utilize all the credits during the year you put the building "in service."

One other important requirement is that you must either own the building (or a portion of it) or have a lease that extends at least thirty-one years. This can and usually does include options. Sometimes, if you have a recalcitrant landlord, you can work out a way to share the credits with him. This obviously has a mutually beneficial effect.

Many states have accessory credit incentives that dovetail nicely with the federal credits. In Colorado, many cities have a state-sponsored "Enterprise Zone." At Wynkoop, we receive a $500 state credit for every new employee position we create. For the first two years, we receive an additional $200 for every employee for whom we pay at least 50 percent of their health insurance. As we are now up to 80 employees, this has been a very important incentive. Although the Enterprise Zone includes more than just the Historic District, that is a very large part of it.

In addition, Colorado has a specifically historic tax credit that provides a state credit worth 10 percent of the federal credit (and so is worth 2 percent of renovation expenditures).

There are some restrictions to these credits, especially in terms of maintaining the exterior appearance of the building as much as is possible. Representatives of the National Park Service are the final arbiters of what is and is not permitted, and so far we have found them exceedingly easy to work with.

Another advantage of an unrenovated historic structure is that often you have the opportunity to purchase such a building at a considerable discount. Even if you do not have the cash to purchase at the beginning, try to include an option clause in your lease so that once you are fabulously successful you can reap more of the fruits of your success. It is said that more than 95 percent of the millionaires in this country attained their wealth through real estate. The problem with real estate is the risk of speculation. But if you have worked to create a successful business, and are willing to continue working to maintain that success, the risk is largely removed.

Conclusions

I could rattle on indefinitely about the glories and rewards of saving old buildings. There can be negatives as well. Some historic buildings or neighborhoods are in somewhat more risky parts of town. At Wynkoop we have managed to make that work for us, but then our Lower Downtown was not too bad.

Also, to renovate a building from scratch usually requires a fair amount more initial capital. A lower lease rate is not much solace when you are having trouble just raising the money to get started.

John Hickenlooper (left) answers questions during the roundtable discussion after his presentation.

Then, once you have raised the money, there are all the catastrophes that lurk within any renovation project. Unforeseen structural problems, or the ugly specter of asbestos are always close at hand, not to mention other potential or as yet unknown environmental hazards.

To me, these risks seem far outweighed by the rewards, both material and spiritual. In some cases you will be pushing over the first domino to help revitalize an urban center. You will be exposing hopefully thousands of people to the wonder of historic buildings and the community's heritage. It is an interesting generality that brewpub entrepreneurs seem to share a common interest in promoting a better world. (Perhaps that's why so many ex-geologist's are attracted to the brewpub world, but that's a different story.)

Brewpubs are a unique opportunity to help save historic buildings. Each brewpub that is built in a shopping mall or a high-rise lobby dilutes that opportunity and weakens the gestalt of the whole endeavor. The brewpub movement is based upon full flavor. An old building is the only way to really savor that flavor.

John Hickenlooper and three partners opened the Wynkoop Brewing Company in Denver, Colorado, is 1988. He helped design and open Coopersmith Pub and Brewing in Fort Collins, Colorado, in 1989, and is presently working with local partners to open brewpubs in Colorado Springs, Lincoln, Nebraska, and Rapid City, South Dakota. He has a fetish for old buildings and fresh beer.

Chapter *4.*

ANGELS AND VULTURES: THE SEARCH FOR FINANCING

*Stephen Dinehart III,
Chicago Brewing Co.*

In starting a business—any business—one faces a series of hurdles. The first hurdle, however, that of financing, is the highest (or seemingly so). Your financial resources dictate your ability to open a business, sustain it during the early years and grow it over time.

Some people call the beer and restaurant business competitive, but compared to the money market, it is tee ball versus the National League. For most of us, raising money tests the full range of our social and intellectual skills. One needs personality, street and book smarts, persuasiveness, fortitude, and tenacity. In addition to these personal traits, one needs to prepare, train for the market, know the players, and formulate a game plan.

Preparation: Training to Face Darwinism in the Capital Markets

Preparation is of utmost importance when you are trying to raise money. Preparation entails knowing the money market, knowing what to say, knowing the answers to questions unasked, and knowing how to communicate what and to whom. The first step

in preparation is to know yourself and where you are going. The best tool for this is the business plan. One must understand that with many capital sources, the first impression beyond a brief telephone call will be with a written document, usually the business plan. The business plan is probably the most important document you will ever prepare for your business. It will serve as an organizer of your thoughts, communicate your vision of the business to others, and provide an anchor for your decisions when the forest is lost in the trees.

The business plan is a document of art. It must thoroughly explain the business — its economic viability and future. It must be simple and concise, but thorough. It is as much a sales tool as a descriptive piece. It must excite and educate.

The business plan needs to answer four basic questions for an investor:
1. Is the business a viable concept?
2. Is the management team competent?
3. Does the business look economically viable?
4. Are the returns adequate?

In answering the first of these questions, one notes that the concept viability of a craft brewery is easier to convey today than it was five or ten years ago since the industry is now established. Nevertheless, many investors are skeptical, and therefore the business plan should hit several points. First, the idea of making beer is romantic and that romance should be played up. Second, statistical evidence exists—and should presented—that this segment of the beer industry is established and growing. The statistics published by the Institute for Brewing Studies are very useful for proving this point.

Finally, concept viability is established by the fact that firms are not only making great beer but are also making money. This point is the true indication of concept viability. Making great beer is art, but making money is business. Unfortunately, this point is the hardest to establish. The financial success of an entity can be established only for public companies, and there are very few such breweries. Of the few I have looked at, none are making money yet. Therefore, I use as the best financial success indicator available, the lack of business failures relative to most small businesses.

Management competence is the second factor. Despite the importance of numbers, they are inevitably discounted. I have heard a number of investors note that the most crucial variable in a project is people, so assemble a good team. Because you are opening a brewery, you must show that your team possesses brewing competency. Many investors will ask for a sample of your recipe. It would be wise to provide them with some pilot brew. It is as close to bricks and mortar as you will come. Don't be shy; note your skills and accomplishments, and demonstrate experience. Chicago Brewing Company had its own particular pitfall. We were a family, blow number one. One venture capital group we spoke to laughed at the concept of investing in a family-run brewery. Upon further investigation, it offered to invest $1.5 million with certain caveats.

The third and fourth components address showing that your particular brewery is economically viable. Given that anyone can generate spreadsheets these days, you need a spreadsheet and it needs to be good. Account for all costs including depreciation and amortization. Generate several sets of figures — a cash flow breakeven, your real expectations, a worse-case and best-case scenario. Remember that any set of figures you show will be discounted, so make one set very high, for example showing a 40 to 50 percent internal rate of return (IRR) over six years. Then add a low set showing a 20 to 25 percent IRR. I hope the lower one is more in line with your real expectations. I saw one plan that projected sales of 20,000 barrels per year after one year. Others use only success stories as examples such as Hood River or Boston Beer Company. Personally, I thought my projections based on West coast numbers were reasonable. Unfortunately, microbreweries are relatively new in the Midwest and the learning curve must be addressed. As for returns, a person can double his money in U.S. treasury notes over ten years, so he expects to at least double this return on your business, due to his risk. Most venture capital firms are looking for average (and I emphasize average) returns of 25 percent so you had better be showing 35 to 45 percent returns.

Once you have your first business plan, you need to get outside advice on your numbers. The amount of input you need will depend on your competency. You may need only quick internal consistency checks by an accountant or a full projection creation. I don't recommend the latter; it costs too much and you learn nothing. Do your own numbers, have them reviewed, and then tell three or four accountants that you'll give them business if they line up investors for you. They will all say they have investors, but use your business as a carrot to get them to follow through. Ultimately, you will need an accounting firm on board to provide accounting help.

The second critical support is legal council on the question of structure. But remember, just as there are incompetent brewers or entrepreneurs, there are incompetent lawyers. One "brewery lawyer" asked me what the ATF regulations meant. One of the brewpub pioneers in my area lost control of his project because of bad lawyering and lousy legal structure. Remember, your legal structure will define your control today and later, as well as your ability to grow the business and raise money. And remember the power of incentives; have your lawyer design *disincentives* into your structure for your removal except for gross negligence.

Regarding structure, your options are fairly straight forward; they are proprietorship, a corporation, an "S" corporation, and a partnership. The particular structure you choose will reflect your needs for money, liability, protection, and control. Don't settle on a structure until you decide who is raising your money. Your particular money raiser may want a certain form of structure for the offering. Decide before you invest $10,000 to $70,000 in legal work.

Financing Sources: The Topology of Getting from Here to There

A business plan will be pitched to multiple financing sources. To effectively market to these sources, you need to understand the background of each.

Banks. We all think of banks first when we need money. Bank money is available if you already have money. Collateral is the name of the game. The collateral value of anything you buy will be discounted, and that discount is known as a *haircut*. Collateral value for new equipment may be 80 percent, for used equipment 50 percent, for leasehold improvements 20 percent, and for inventory 10 percent. So you can't build a brewery on a bank's money unless you have a house or some other investment to put up as insurance. Many of the brewery equipment manufacturers can hook you up with a finance or lease arrangement for equipment or "hard assets," but that's your easiest raise.

Family and friends. Most professionals advise to steering clear of family and friends, but for most of us, they are the easiest source of funds. They know you and your talents, but remember that in asking for money, you are adding new dimensions to your relationship. You must be able to take a "no" gracefully. Friends and family may be able to provide seed money but generally little more.

Accredited investors. Accredited investors have a particular meaning in the context of securities law. These are individuals whom the SEC has declared as being "financially sophisticated" based on their income or net worth. Therefore, they don't have to have all the disclosure required for investment by widows and orphans. *Angels*, as accredited investors are called, are the best source of capital if you can tap them. They expect a high rate of return, but not too high. They generally allow you to have control and they can invest in large chunks.

The problem is accessing these individuals. Unsolicited requests are technically a no-no and generally won't elicit a response anyway. The best access to these angels is through an established broker/dealer (B/D). An established B/D will have developed relationships and hopefully be a trusted financial adviser. He or she will cost you 10 percent of the money raised, plus he may want a *backend* — a percentage of ownership based on the raise.

Institutional investors. Institutional investors are your last hope for money and are usually pension funds that place a portion of their money in "venture deals." These investors are usually best accessed via venture capital companies. Venture groups are the most demanding of investors. These *vultures*, as they are called, give money, but demand flesh. Performance criteria are tight. Returns are expected to be high. Also, some management control must be ceded to the venture group. The good news is that venture groups have invested in microbreweries and are making money. The bad news is that the venture market is less than half of what it was last year.

Others. I want to note a number of other sources, including government sources that you should explore.

Small Business Administration (SBA) loans are readily available either through your local banker or a guaranteed lender. Use a guaranteed lender for quick approval; they charge high interest, but they'll take your risk.

Small Business Investment Companies (SBIC) are the SBA's answer to venture firms. They operate as venture firms but are partially government funded. Funding is often available.

State/Local Governments may offer block grant funds, low-interest loans, etc.

Strategic Alliances through joint ventures are alive and well and should be explored if proper introductions can be made.

Public Offering is the final option. This is the most costly of raises. Up-front legal costs may be $70,000 to $100,000. In addition, you really want a B/D to serve as an underwriter. The Initial Public Offering (IPO) market is hot today, but in six months, who knows. A blind or concept IPO is hard to pull off, but it can be done.

Intra State Offering should also be explored and may be less costly if you can avoid SEC requirements.

The Chicago Brewing Experience

Our experience raising money for CBC may be instructive. We first started the process of raising money under the naive notion that banks would lend 90 percent on a project. One individual in our original group contended that restaurants were financed this way. Using this information and our initial business plan, we approached several banks and were politely told that a 10 percent equity stake in the project represented severe underfunding.

After this deadend, our accountant suggested that we speak to a lawyer about limited partnerships. We met with this lawyer and after about three months had an offering document for $1.6 million in limited partnership units. After about four months worth of sales effort, we had placed only about $500,000 in units. Our critical mistake at this juncture was not using a licensed B/D for such a large raise. If one is issuing a large equity offering, it is advisable to line up a licensed B/D to develop the package in conjunction with your lawyer.

At this point we did some soul searching to arrive at a solution to our funding dilemma. We knew that we could raise some money using different techniques. Therefore, we decided to use a composite approach. We raised equity funding from our seed money and supplemented that with money from most of the individuals interested in our first limited partnership offering. In addition, the owner of the equipment we were purchasing agreed to take partial payment in equity. Using this equity base, we were able to line up an SBA-guaranteed loan with additional low-interest loan money from the state. This integrated approach was ultimately successful.

Conclusion

We initially approached our fundraising from the perspective that a great idea will draw money. This was a naive vision and such an approach is doomed to fail.

The reality is that the money market is the most competitive market you will ever face. You are selling a concept, and without proper preparation, you will never succeed.

Several lessons came from our experience. First, always maintain multiple efforts because such an approach will assure the quickest results. Second, try everything; take no one's experience as gospel. We didn't try an SBA loan because we had heard it would take too long, yet ultimately it was our quickest form of financing. Third, network, network, network. People yield results, and the more people who know about your offering, the more likely you are to succeed. Finally, don't be cheap. It costs money to raise money. Use a financial adviser or a licensed B/D, and agree to pay whatever is necessary. Just make sure the fee is based on actual funds raised. His or her rolodex of investors may only be paper, but it is paper made of gold.

Stephen Dinehart III is the founder and president of the Chicago Brewing Company, began in 1989. It is Illinois' largest brewery and the only commercial brewery located in Chicago. The Dinehart family has deep roots in the brewing industry; it operated the Dinehardt Brewery in Weimar, Germany until World War II. In addition to the brewery, Stephen maintains an avocation as Senior Economist at the Chicago Board of Trade. He holds graduate degrees in agricultural economics and economics from Michigan State University.

Chapter 5.

ASSURING THE BEST BEER

*Richard Rench Ph.D.,
Upper Canada Brewing Co.*

I will begin this presentation on beer quality and what the brewer can do to ensure that the customer receives beer in its best possible condition by defining quality as "when the customer comes back not the beer."

Many people who have had the opportunity to taste fresh beer from a bright beer tank agree that beer is at its best then. From that point on, most subsequent influences on the beer tend to be detrimental to its quality. Some of the influences are beyond the brewer's control; for example, a customer may place his beer in the trunk of his car during a heatwave or the middle of winter. There are, however, many measures a brewer can take to reduce or eliminate problems that can harmfully affect beer after filtration. Some of these measures take place in the brewhouse, and others during fermentation, maturation or packaging. I will attempt to explain them in simple, cost-justifiable ways. Often the simplest solution is maintaining good control and adherence to well-tested procedures.

A beer tends to be judged first by its appearance, which includes assessing its head, clarity and color; we tend to taste

initially with our eyes. Next, a beer is judged by its aroma and taste, and then its aftertaste and the amount of cling on the glass. These are the parameters about which the brewer is most concerned. Whereas aroma and taste are difficult to measure, the other parameters can at least be defined and repeatedly checked against predetermined specifications. Customer loyalty is generated by supplying him with a consistently good product. Once the criteria for judging a beer is established, the brewer must adhere to them and not bend to commercial pressures for short-term gain when the product does not meet specifications.

Table 1
Parameters for a German-style Lager and an English-style Ale

	Lager	Pale Ale
Alcohol	5.0 + 0.3	4.8 + 0.3
Color	10.0 + 2.0	20 + 2.0
Carbon Dioxide	2.5 + 0.2	2.5 + 0.2
Head Retention	> 120 secs	>100 secs
Air Content	< 1 ml/341 ml	< 1 ml/341ml

Table 1 illustrates some of the more easily measurable parameters for a German-style lager and an English-style pale ale. You will notice that there is a defined range of parameters. These should be achievable from a production standpoint, but they depend on the accuracy or repeatability of the test.

Alcohol Percent

The percentage of alcohol can be determined fairly easily by distillation, but the errors inherent in the method are plus or minus 0.3 percent for a beer of 5 percent alcohol. More sophisticated methods such as gas liquid chromatography are more accurate and faster, but the equipment is costly and requires a skilled operator. It is necessary to routinely measure the alcohol content of a beer in order to ensure that the brewer is producing what he claims and to provide the data on which revenue duty (tax) is calculated. In small breweries that do not use high-gravity brewing and dilution techniques, control is best maintained by achieving the correct collection gravity.

Color

Beer color can readily be determined by Lovibond comparative discs or a spectrophotometer. Many people associate darker beer colors with increased strength. Once the customer has become accustomed to a beer being a certain color, it is very difficult to persuade him that there is not something wrong with the product when its color is different. This is one reason for adhering to one's specifications. Color can easily be increased in the bright beer tank by adding a calculated amount of a caramel solution. Caramel, however, can be considered an additive, and so it is better either to get the color right in the brewhouse by adding black malt or to blend beers from the bright beer bank.

Clarity

Beer clarity can be determined by hazemeters that measure the amount of light scattered at set angles. For example, a hazemeter can measure the light scattered at 90 degrees or at 30 degrees. (See Table 2.) Particles in solution reflect light shining at different angles depending on their size, and so hazemeters measure differ-

RICHARD RENCH PH.D. 51

Table 2
Using A Hazemeter

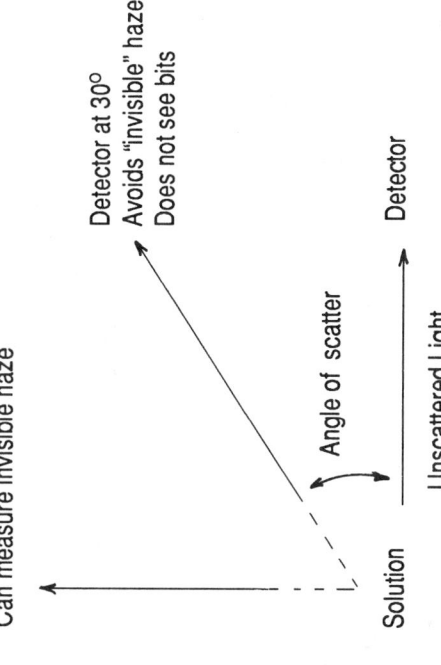

ent-sized particles. Unfortunately, the results do not always concur, and it is quite possible to have a visibly bright beer with an unacceptable haze level because of the presence of fine particles (as can occur with the 90-degree meter). Or a beer that may appear to meet the specificiations may have "bits" in it. The simplest solution to this apparent dilemma is to view the beer against a black-and-white background created by simply placing a piece of black tape on a florescent tube. Particles and casts can easily be seen against the black background, and a judgment can be made. This can save spending several thousand dollars on a piece of equipment, and it is more representative of how consumers judge the beer.

Having identified a means for determining the haze level, it is more than a little frustrating to discover that the beer has developed a haze while it is in the trade. Preventing this from happening requires understanding how hazes are caused. (See Table 3.) There are two major causes of haze, biological and non-biological. Biological hazes are normally associated with anaerobic bacterial infections such as lactobacillus, which under unfavorable conditions such as warm temperatures, may result in sedimentation. Unfortunately, lactobacillus enjoys the same conditions as many brewery yeasts and is present in most breweries despite stringent efforts to remove it. Concentrating one's efforts on good sanitary cleaning and changing the yeast culture is essential in preventing major problems. But also, ensuring that the level of lactobacillus present at the end of maturation is low enough not to subsequently create a problem in the trade is worth the cost.

If it is assured that the packaged beer will not be kept at temperatures above 48 degrees F (8 degrees C), then a beer with an anaerobic bacterial count of up to one cell per ml will probably be stable for up to six weeks. The test for this requires filtering at least 100 ml of beer through a filter disc under anaerobic conditions, and then incubating it at 82 degrees F (28 degrees C) for three days on

Table 3
Causes and Control of Haze

Biological
    Aerobic   Acetic Acid Bacteria
    Anaerobic   Lactic Acid Bacteria
                          Zymomonas
                          Wild yeast
    Control: Good hygiene
                    Regular change of yeast culture
Nonbiological
    Reactions of proteins and polyphenols
    Control: Brewhouse
                    Maturation
                    Filtration
                    Packaging

Biological Hazes

48 degrees F (8 degrees C) : Maximum of 1 Anaerobic Cell per ml
More than 6 weeks :   Less than 1 Cell Per 200 ml

Control: Pasteurization
                Absolute filtration
Tests:
1) 82 degrees F (28 degrees C) for 3 days on defined media
2) Forcing Test - Bottle Held at 77 degrees F (25 degrees C) for 28 Days
3) Integrity Tester for Cartridges

Nonbiological Hazes

Proteins and polyphenols or proanthocyanogens result in haze
Sources: Malt and hops extracted in brewhouse
Factors   Concentration
             Temperature
             Metal Ions
             Oxygen

Control of Nonbiological Hazes

1. Barley Variety Selection — Low Proanthocyanogen and Nitrogen
2. Low Mash Temperature and pH — 122 degrees F (50 degrees C) for Proteolysis
3. Adjuncts Dilute Nitrogen
4. Vigorous Boil for 90 minutes at 212 degrees F (100 degrees C)
5. Bright Worts — At Wort Run-Off (e.g., Lautering)
   At Trub Removal (e.g., Whirlpool)
6. Store Beer at 32 degrees F (0 degrees C), or Less, for 7 Days

Corrective Measures

Enzymes
Protein Absorbants
    Silica Gels
    Bentonite
    Tannins
Anthocyanogen Removal
    PVPP
Identify and eliminate Sources of heavy metals
    Iron (.5 ppm Plus)
    Copper (.5 ppm Plus)
    Tin

a defined media. However, if the conditions after packaging are beyond the control of the brewer, then tighter standards are required. For bottled beer, it is not unreasonable to expect the in-package anaerobic bacterial count to be less than one cell in 200 ml. This is beyond the capability of most diatomaceous earth and sterile pad systems.

Pasteurization can kill all bacteria, but the equipment tends to be capital intensive with high maintenance and operating costs. But of greater importance, pasteurization can impair the beer's taste. Absolute filtration cartridges can be a more cost-effective solution that produces beer with extremely low bacterial counts without detriment to the flavor. It is possible to determine if the cartridges are intact—if they have holes that might let bacteria through—with an integrity tester, but the testers are expensive. As a measure of the effectiveness of a pasteurization or filtration system, there should be no signs of a sediment in a bottled beer left for twenty-eight days in a room at 77 degrees F (25 degrees C). Microbiological tests should also be performed. The advantages of pasteurization and filtration are that a brewer can ship the beer without having to wait for the microbiological plate result and won't waste effort packaging a product that may later be returned.

Non-biological hazes tend to be formed by the complexing of malt proteins with proanthocyanogens or polyphenols derived from hops and malt. These materials are formed during mashing and wort boiling, and the reactions continue during cold storage. The rate of formation depends on the concentration of the two main components, plus the temperature and the presence of metal ions and oxygen. Since the hazes develop over time, it is quite possible for the beer to be bright at filtration and then for the haze to develop in final package over the next months. It is difficult to predict, or match the conditions that beer is subjected to in the trade. It is therefore better to do things correctly during the brewing process rather than take corrective actions later.

Work is ongoing to develop malting grades of barley that have low levels of proanthocyanogens, but so far the yields have been low and farmers have found the proposition unattractive. Likewise, low nitrogen barley would be beneficial, but farmers are not receiving sufficient financial incentive to produce it on a commercial scale. In the brewhouse, low mash temperatures of 122 degrees F (50 degrees C) favor proteolysis, which helps reduce the amount of high molecular weight proteins. A lower mash pH is desirable because tannins, which are the precursors of haze-forming materials, are less soluble at lower pH values. Adjuncts such as rice have low nitrogen levels and thus act as nitrogen diluents, which favor stability.

The benefits of a good vigorous boil cannot be overemphasized since boiling leads to a good hot break formation. Classically, wort should be boiled for ninety minutes at 212 degrees F (100 degrees C). More modern brewing systems allow for considerable reductions in the time and hence lead to energy savings, but beers produced from these systems may require more treatments during maturation. It is essential to have equipment that effectively removes the hot break, i.e., a well-designed whirlpool. The addition of copper finings at the end of wort boiling can help trub compaction, which results in less carry-over of solid material and therefore brighter worts. The more trub that can be removed in the brewhouse, the better, since that means there will be less protein to remove at maturation and filtration and less potential for hazes to form after packaging.

The other essential step in ensuring good stability is storing the beer at less than 32 degrees F (0 degrees C) for seven days to effectively remove chillhazes and prevent temperature pick-up during subsequent filtration. The disadvantage of this process is high refrigeration cost and poor tank utilization. It is hardly surprising that brewers have sought ways of reducing storage time without detriment to the clarity and shelf-life of the beer. The attempts have concentrated on reducing the protein content of the beer, or the polyphenol and anthocyanogen content. Also, enzymes such as Papain—a protease extracted from the latex of the papaya plant—have been used. The action of enzymes at freezing temperatures is somewhat limited but could be of benefit in nonpasteurized beers. However, many proteases are nonspecific and may well hydrolyze glycoproteins associated with head retention as well as the haze precursors. The use of protein absorbants such as silica gels added directly to the maturation tank or as part of the body feed may be an effective aid to achieving stability.

The anthocyanogen portion of haze-forming materials may be removed using Polyvinyl polypyrrolidone (more commonly referred to as PVPP). PVPP can be added to maturation tank but with the disadvantage that it is lost with the tank bottoms. PVPP is expensive and can be recovered and regenerated within specialized filtration systems or special filter pads, but the initial capital outlay for such systems is substantial.

Metal ions such as iron, copper and tin are a well-known cause of haze formation. Diatomaceous earth has been known to be a source of iron and should occasionally be checked or a certificate of analysis sought on batch deliveries. However, a far more likely reason for iron pick-up is mild steel coming in contact with the beer at some stage. Stainless steel is considerably more expensive than mild steel, but its value is certainly well proven. Pump heads, valves and fittings should be stainless steel. Occasional surveys of the plant can be very rewarding; in emergencies, materials or equipment may not be so carefully considered.

Beer Foam

Another factor a consumer notices before he picks up his glass is the presence or absence of a good head and tight foam. Many people find it very satisfying to drink through the foam and then see the cling left on the glass. Unfortunately, a bartender can undo the good work of the brewer and his fine intentions by not adequately rinsing detergent from the glasses. The brewer can only hope this is not the case. Although not very sophisticated, an easy method for

Table 4
Beer Foam

Simple Test	1 cm. (1/2 inch) Head to Remain 120 secs.
Foam Positives	Glycoproteins CO_2 or N Limit Beer Transfers/Agitation
Foam Negatives	Extensive Wort Boiling Lipids Antifoam Detergents

Improving Beer Foam

Methods:	High Carbon Dioxide High Nitrogen Wheat in Grist Propylene Glycol Alginate (P.G.A.) Zinc Sulfate (2 ppm.)

determining the head retention value is to pour a standard amount of beer (such as bottleful) into a straight-sided pint glass and determine the amount of foam remaining after awhile. (See Table 4.) At least 1 cm of foam should remain for more than 120 seconds. Very sophisticated methods involving filming the collapse of the foam with a video camera and interpreting the results with a computer are in the development stage, and the results are said to be reproducible. It remains to be seen if many brewers adopt such tests.

Beer foam is a function of two factors: the glycoproteins derived from the malt and the gas content of the beer. Unfortunately, many of the procedures beneficial to achieving clarity and reducing haze-forming potential are detrimental to producing beers with good head. For example, extensive wort boiling improves the nonbiological stability of beer but helps destroy beer foam materials. A sensible balance can be achieved, and there are many other procedures for obtaining the desired results. For example, when transferring beer, the system should be designed to reduce the amount of agitation. Pumps should be switched off when not in use rather than be allowed to pump a small amount of beer against a dead end. The number of transfers should be minimized. In this sense, the concept of unitanks — where the same vessel is used for fermenting and maturing — is advantageous for helping preserve beer foam. The presence of head negative material (i.e., lipids, antifoam and detergents) can be extremely detrimental to foam stability at levels as low as 1 ppm.

The carbon dioxide content of a beer can be increased to help improve foam, but high levels of carbon dioxide can make the beer difficult to package, dispense and consume in volume. As an alternative gas, nitrogen is finding favor with many large brewers. Nitrogen forms smaller, more tightly-knit bubbles that decay at slower rates to give better head and improved cling in the glass. It is inert and can be used in gas washing beer or removing oxygen from the cutting liquor in high-gravity brewing. However, its use may not be acceptable or cost-justifiable for many smaller breweries. The correct balance of the gases has to be found and another test has to be made. Using a mixture of the two gases at dispense for draft beer may be a simpler system.

The brewer can help preserve beer foam by incorporating materials such as wheat into the grist. Wheat can be added as malted wheat such as that used in wheat beers. Alternatively, micronized wheat or wheat flour can form part of the mash. The proportion of such adjuncts should be determined with care since adjuncts can cause problems during wort run-off and beer filtration. Major brewers have tried adding materials at filtration to enhance and stabilize foam. Propylene glycol alginate, derived from certain seaweeds, is an effective but expensive material that enhances beer foam and the cling in the glass. Zinc sulfate at levels of 2 ppm helps preserve beer foam, but controlling the rate of dosage requires good laboratory back-up. Beers using such materials tend to be of the "chemical" type, and it is certainly difficult to call them "all-natural."

Beer Flavor

Perhaps the most difficult parameter to measure, the most subjective, and yet probably the most important, is beer flavor. We all have opinions, and we all perceive different flavors at different flavor threshholds. Indeed, we often do not like certain beer styles even when they are well-produced. We can usually agree, however, if beer flavors have changed and become stale. Stale flavors develop with time. The rate of their formation depends on the amount of oxygen that gets into the beer after fermentation, the temperature of storage (higher temperatures accelerate the reactions), and the concentration of precursor materials. With time, there is also a shift in the sweetness to bitterness balance as the sensory bitterness steadily decreases.

The three most notable unpleasant flavors that develop are ribes or catty, sweet/butterscotch, and cardboard/papery flavors. The ribes flavor increases rapidly and then decreases slowly. The sweet/butterscotch flavor generally increases gradually and some people find it quite pleasant. The most unacceptable flavor is the cardboard/papery one because it is associated with a loss in beer drinkability. Most people can detect it even if they cannot define it, and they end up drinking less or switching to something else.

The cardboard flavor is associated with certain aldehydes—generally medium-chain length, saturated alpha-beta, unsaturated aldehydes. Their source is lipid material, such as Linoleic acid,

Table 5
Stale Flavors

Time Dependent
Amount of Oxygen Pick-up Post Fermentation
Temperature of Storage
Concentration of Precoursors

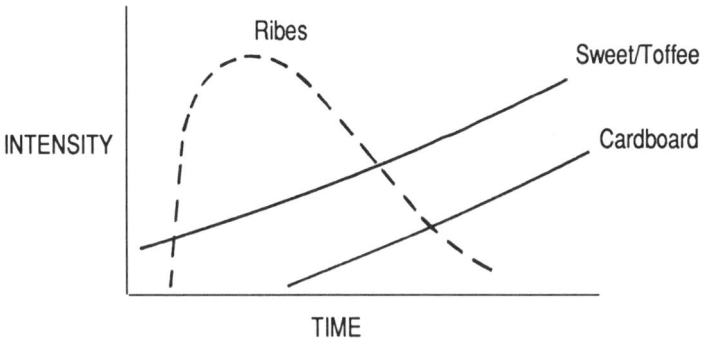

Control of Stale Flavors

Bright Worts	Lower in Lipids
Sparge Temps	165-172 degrees F (74-78 degrees C)
Crystal Malt	
Wort Seperation Procedure and Plant Desgn	Keep Oxygen Out

derived from the brewhouse. A simplified description of the formation is shown in Table 5. Thus, the brewer can prevent flavor deterioration in the trade by reducing the amount of lipid materials extracted during wort production. The brewers of by-gone times concentrated their efforts and insisted on producing bright worts

Table 6
Oxidation of Linoleic Acid

Linoleic Acid
↓
Intermediates
↓
Tri-Hydroxyoctadecenoic Acid
↓ eg.

$$CH_3(CH_2)_4 \overset{OH}{\underset{OH}{\wedge\wedge\wedge}} \overset{OH}{} (CH_2)_7 CO_2H$$

↓

Saturated and Unsaturated Aldehydes

from the mash-tun—and with good reason: cloudy worts tend to be high in lipid content. (See Table 6.) Ensuring that consistent sparge temperatures in the range of 165 to 172 degrees F (74 to 78 degrees C) are achieved also minimizes lipid carry-over. It has been found that crystal malt, when it is part of the grist, produces beer less prone to staling. It is of benefit to beer flavor to reduce the amount of carbonyls in wort by adhering to good mashing and wort separation techniques, and to ensure that wort is not held at high temperatures for long periods of time to limit the formation of Maillard reaction products and related substances such as carbonyls.

Avoiding Oxygen Pick-Up

So far, I have briefly alluded to the undesirable presence of oxygen. In essence, oxygen is only required in controlled amounts at the start of fermentation to ensure that the yeast cells produce more cell wall material and that a successful primary fermentation ensues. At all other times, oxygen pick-up is detrimental, and procedures and equipment should be designed to minimize it. Modern lauter tun design concentrates on introducing worts at the bottom of the vessel. Mash mixer agitators have for some time been designed to prevent the entrapment of air. Wort boiling systems are designed to keep air out to reduce color pick-up.

However, after primary fermentation, the need to keep air out is even more important, and plant failure or a brewer's bad decision can have disastrous consequences. For example, one brewery that tried to package its beer using air instead of carbon dioxide for its first production batch (the carbon dioxide was late in arriving) never did recover. The beer had to be recalled after one week because of substantial flavor changes. Unfortunately, the brewery shut within two years. For many people, their first experience with the brewery's product was so memorable that they did not want to repeat it.

First and foremost, every effort must be made to keep air out of beer, and I will describe some of the more likely sources of pick-up and the necessary corrective action. (See Table 7.) Most of the pick-up occurs when beer is being transferred. The primary sources are the seals of pumps and loose hose connections. If beer can get out, albeit in a slow leak, then air can get in. Thus, checking the seals for any beer leaks and repairing pinhole leaks or hairline cracks is beneficial. Equipment should be designed to minimize turbulence particularly if there is no inert gas cover. Fill and flush vessels thoroughly with carbon dioxide or nitrogen before commencing a transfer; this includes maturation tanks as well as bright

Table 7
Sources of Air/Oxygen Pickup

Beer Transfers
Pump Seals + Hose Connections
Plant Design + Procedures
Filter Powder
Filling Operations

Ways to Minimize Air/Oxygen Pickup

Procedures - Carbon Dioxide Flush
Operator Awareness
Maintenance Program
In-Plant Monitoring (e.g. D.O. Meter)
Additives
    Sulfide Dioxide
    Vitamin C (ascorbic acid) at 5 gms/HL

beer tanks. When designing a plant, it is worthwhile to consider using the same vessel for fermentation and maturation to minimize beer transfers.

Oxygen pick-up is inevitable within a diatomaceous earth filtration system. Air is entrained between the particles, but at least the agitator can be designed to minimize air pick-up. While operating these filters, the vent ports should regularly be flushed to keep the filter full of beer. The seals of bottle filler tubes should routinely be changed. It is essential to ensure that the jetter or tapper on the filler is working, so that any surplus air is removed from the container prior to capping. It is also worthwhile to educate employees on the dangers of air in beer and let them taste a very oxidized product. A good, in-house maintenance program can ensure that seals and gaskets are changed before they disintegrate.

A meter to measure dissolved oxygen can be a very useful tool for identifying where air pick-up is occurring. However, using the dissolved content as part of the specification for final packaged goods can be misleading because the dissolved oxygen content changes with time, as the oxygen is used up. In other words, the damage may already have been done before the final, in-package result is known. A dissolved oxygen meter is a far more powerful tool when it is used routinely after each beer transfer or as part of a survey to highlight problem areas.

Stabilizers

Various materials can be added to beer to enhance its stability in the final package. Sulfur dioxide added as sodium metabisulfite at the end of fermentation is effective, but the beer may develop unpleasant sulfidic aromas. Also, some people have allergic reactions to sulfite, so if it is used at rates above 10 ppm, the beer label may have to state its presense even though the actual sulfite level in the final package is less. Ascorbic acid, which is better known as vitamin C, can be added during maturation or filtration at rates of 5 mg per hectoliter as an effective antioxidant. But the customer then may perceive the beer as being "chemical." It is far better to design and operate equipment to prevent air ingress from occurring rather than mopping it up later.

Conclusion

Brewing can be a simple procedure, and very good beer that stands up well in the trade can be made without using chemicals or preservatives. In essence, the more that is added to beer, the greater the chance for error and for increasing the need for more tests. The brewer must be vigilant, however, to routinely check raw materials and their certificates of analysis to see that established procedures are followed, and to ensure that the plant is in good working order. Explaining to employees the dangers of bad practices can be very worthwhile since personnel can be encouraged to report anomalies as they occur, so that corrective action can immediately be taken. The brewer should inform himself or herself of all trade complaints; I find that handling them directly saves time and creates an excellent impression for the customer.

I have deliberately avoided talking about the costs involved in ensuring that beer will stand up well in the trade. It is essential that the brewer produce consistently good products that do not deteriorate prematurely. It is very easy to spend a lot of money on sophisticated equipment and on quality control in general, but this does not necessarily ensure that the beer will not be returned. Rather, good equipment and procedures will enable problem areas to be identified and will become more necessary as the process gets more complicated.

I believe, however, that if brewing is kept simple and the well-tried procedures are adhered to, then a brewer can produce a quality beer with a good shelf-life with only a small financial outlay for quality control. This helps keep costs down and ensures that the customer comes back, and not the beer.

Richard Rench, Ph.D., is brewmaster at the Upper Canada Brewing Company in Toronto, Canada, where as vice president in charge of brewing, he is responsible for all aspects of production. He graduated from the University of Birmingham in the United Kingdom with a doctorate in biochemistry. He holds a diploma from the Institute of Brewing in London and is a current member of the Master Brewers Association of the Americas.

Chapter 6.

INSURANCE FOR MICROBREWERIES

*Peter Whalen,
Goggins and Whalen Insurance Agency*

Most business owners have little idea exactly how to go about searching for the best insurance program available in the marketplace. They usually respond to the many solicitations they receive from local agencies and base their decision solely, or at least primarily on price. Another consideration is how much time it will take to get an insurance program. Many brewery owners do not enjoy dealing with insurance, and therefore, they try to spend as little time as possible talking to insurance agents. Yet, obtaining adequate insurance coverage is one of the most important functions of a business manager. It is my goal to help you understand how best to go about purchasing sufficient insurance protection at an affordable price.

The first step in the process of getting the appropriate insurance is analyzing what amount of coverages and liability limits are required for microbreweries and brewpubs. Table 1 shows a checklist of coverages you can use when next you shop for insurance. The checklist should be completed sixty to ninety days prior to the expiration of your current policy. If you properly complete the checklist, the majority of your analysis will be done.

Coverage Checklist

A.) Property Per Location   Limit
    1.) Building (if applicable)   _____
    2.) Contents   _____
    3.) Loss of Income   _____
    4.) Extra Expense   _____
    5.) Exterior Signs   _____
    6.) Food & Beer Spoilage   _____
    7.) Money & Securities   _____
    8.) Employee Dishonesty   _____
    9.) Glass (measurements)   _____

B.) Liability (Premises & Product)   _____
C.) Liquor Liability   _____
D.) Workman's Compensation (payroll) _____
E.) Boiler & Machinery   _____
F.) Automobile (schedule of vehicles)   _____
G.) Bonds (state & federal requirements) _____
H.) Umbrella Liability   _____

    Although I don't plan to go over each item on the checklist, I do want to discuss the importance of researching the liability limits you choose because this information will serve as the foundation of your insurance program. If this first step is done inaccurately, your insurance program will always fall short of its intention.

    Determining the proper limit of contents coverage can be done by no one but you. This figure should equal the sum of the costs of replicating everything within the walls of your brewery for which it would be your financial responsibility to replace in the event of a total loss. The figure should include tenants' improvements and betterments. Most of you are fortunate in that your businesses are new and you are very aware of what you had to invest in order to begin operating. I cannot overemphasize the importance of choosing an accurate figure here.

The only other limit that may take a considerable amount of your time to determine is loss of income. This coverage provides you with funds to pay any on-going expenses in addition to any profits you would lose were your brewery to be shut down due to a covered loss. To arrive at an adequate figure, you need to examine your monthly expenses and list those you would still have if your brewery were closed down. Debt service, managerial salaries and utilities are good examples.

Add to this number the amount of profits you would lose and then multiply this sum by the number of months it would take to rebuild if you had a total loss. The only way to avoid this work is to obtain a policy that offers what is called "actual loss sustained" coverage in which case the insurance company pays actual expenses after the loss as they are incurred, without any predetermined limit.

Once you have completed the checklist, you should put together a list of specifications such as the one shown in Table 2. I took this from a restaurant/banquet facility I recently worked on. The owner produced this document without any assistance from an insurance agent. As a result of his diligence, he avoided constant phone calls from agents trying to obtain the information necessary to develop a quotation.

Pertinent information that should be included on the specifications document is annual payroll, annual receipts, square footage of the facility, and a full description of the building.

In addition, you should include three years of loss runs, financial statements or proformas, and details of any of your brewery's programs or unique features that will make your business more attractive to an insurance company. Examples of these are the "Tips" alcohol training program or non-slip surfaces where water tends to gather. The entire purpose of this exercise is to sell yourself to the insurer. Underwriters are very impressed with

Insurance Guidelines
For Bidding Purposes Only

The Delaneu House
Route 5 at Smith's Ferry
Holyoke, MA 01040
Attention George W. Page, Jr.

Policy period September 1, 1991 - September 1, 1992

SALES

Food	$2,300,000
Beverage	700,000
Total	$3,000,000

PROPERTY
Broad form Comp General Liability
Building 90% co, 1000 deductible, limit 2,400,000
Contents 90% co, 1000 deductible, limit 1,200,000
Business interrupt actual loss sustained 6 months actual loss
Extra expense 100% insurance up to 100,000
Awning - 100 deductible, 15,000 limit
Sign One - 100 deductible, 10,000 limit
Sign Two - 100 deductible, 10,000 limit
Extention of building coverage - 10,000 limit
Fire Protection Equipment Malfunction - 10,000 limit
Valet Parking on Premises Coverage
Scheduled Glass Coverage
Front Doors - 10,000 limit

LIABILITY
Comp Broad Form including Bodily Injury
Damage and Product and Employee Liability
250 deductible on property - 1,000,000 underlying limit including liquor to 1,000,000 underlying limit
Umbrella 2,000,000 above underlying including liquor
Auto/Truck Liability endorsement over motor vehicle underlying

CRIME/FIDELITY
Loss inside premises - 100 deductible, 25,000 limit
Loss outside - 100 deductible, 25,000 limit
Fideltiy Bond - 250 deductible, 25,000 limit

BOILER & MACHINERY
With Boiler - 250 deductible, 1,250,000 limit
Food Spoilage - 250 deductible,

Workman's Comp to be determined

excessive detail, and often this is reflected in their pricing of an account.

The one thing most of you will never lack is interest from insurance agents who want an opportunity to insure your brewery. Since this may uncharted territory for you, let me offer some advice on what to look for.

Preferably, you are dealing with the owner of an agency or a producer or agent who has a long history with his or her agency. Producers have a tendency to move around a lot or even leave the insurance industry altogether. When buying insurance, you don't want to place your account with someone who is not going to be there when you call.

You also want to make sure that the people who are handling your account are well versed and have several years' experience in commercial insurance. Ideally, your insurance agent has a broad base of knowledge and familiarity with your type of operation. The microbrewery industry is still very new, and your agent should be aware of the unique property and liability exposure you face.

Always ask your agent about the quality of the company with which he is placing your business. You want to make sure that the company is large enough and has a financial rating of "A" or "A+"

Denison's Brewpub in Toronto features Bavarian Brewing Equipment, including these five fermentation tanks, from Prinz Luitpold's company.

according to *Best's Key Rating Guide*. Best is a company that rates all insurance companies in the industry.

Finally, inquire how flexible a company is when it receives unusual requests. For example, would your liquor liability coverage follow you if you were to participate in a regional food or beer festival? Unfortunately, even though you might ask, questions like this often are not answered truthfully until it is too late for you to change companies.

Shopping for insurance is not unlike shopping for other consumer goods. The more time you take in investigating the different factors involved, the better you will be able to make an educated decision and the better you will be satisfied with the end result. Remember, be sure you know exactly what you need, so that you will know if you have found it at the end of your search.

Peter Whalen is president of Goggins and Whalen Insurance Agency, Inc. and is a certified insurance counselor and licensed insurance advisor. Sponsored by the Institute for Brewing Studies, he has researched a specialized insurance program for small breweries. Goggins and Whalen is an allied trade member of the Institute for Brewing Studies.

Chapter 7.

ATF AND THE LABEL APPROVAL PROCESS

Jerry Bowerman, Bureau of Alcohol, Tobacco and Firearms

As chief of the famous, if not infamous, Product Compliance Branch of the Bureau of Alcohol, Tobacco and Firearms, (ATF), I and my staff want to work with you to make the label approval process as simple and easy as possible. We process more than 80,000 label applications a year, and so anything that makes the process simple for you, makes it easier for us as well. To that end, I want to explain how label applications are processed by ATF and what we look for when we review your labels. I also want to point out some of the most common mistakes that can bring a simple process to a screeching halt.

More than 90 percent of the 80,000-plus label applications processed last year by the ATF were approved. That may explain why this process is referred to as the "label approval process." We don't like having to disapprove label applications.

The Label Approval Process

The approval process begins when we receive your label application. Label applications received by mail are individually entered into a computer log. This enables us to more easily track

the progress and status of your application. Once the application has been entered into the computer, it is assigned to a Product Compliance Branch specialist for review. This assignment is based on an alphabetical division of work. We strive for consistency in all areas including the working relationship between a specific specialist and a company. However, personnel changes and extreme fluctuations in the numbers of in-coming documents often necessitate reassignment of work.

As background on the process, Product Compliance's staff includes seventeen specialists. Over half of these people devote their time to the review, processing and, as often as possible, approval of label applications. This is extremely complex, technical and demanding work.

Once the specialist receives your application, he or she carefully scrutinizes it. The label is reviewed for compliance with all federal labeling requirements. It must also be reviewed, sometimes with greater concern for misleading or prohibited statements. The initiating specialist is also responsible for ensuring that the form itself is properly completed. Based on this review, the initiating specialist decides whether the label application is approvable. If so, the application is stamped with the director's signature and the date of approval. If the specialist determines that the label is not approvable, he or she completes a correction sheet explaining the problem or problems with the label and/or label application.

In either case, whether the label is approved or denied, the next step in processing is a second level of review by a more experienced specialist. After this second review, the label application is returned to the applicant for correction or issued as a certificate of label approval (COLA). Each certificate, immediately upon final approval, is assigned a unique Document Serial Number, an eleven-digit number that includes the month and year of approval and then microfilmed.

At this point, the applicant's copy (or copies) is mailed to the address indicated in Item 3 of ATF Form 5100.31 (Application/ Certification of Label/Bottle Approval) and ATF's copy is used for computer entry purposes. Information on each and every certificate is maintained in our COLA System. This system provides access, by a variety of fields such as brand name, designations and bottler's name to all microfilmed certificates.

In addition to mail-in labels, we also process labels on a walk-in basis. Industry members and/or their representatives may drop off labels at our office. This "Front Desk" service is open Monday through Friday, 10 a.m. to 12 p.m. and 1 p.m. to 3 p.m. We try to treat dropped-off and mailed-in applications equally. But you should expect a longer turn-around time for mailed in applications, if only because of the time the application spends in transit between your office and ATF. If you have not received your approval, correction sheet or a phone call from us within ten days after you mail in your application, don't hesitate to call us to see what's going on with your application.

Instant Help

As a matter of fact, we've established a "Help Desk" to handle your calls on the status of label applications as well as questions on labeling in general. If you have questions, call us at (202) 927-8140 and ask for the "Help Desk." We'll take care of the problem and/ or get an answer to your question as quickly as we can.

Label Requirements

What do we look for when we review your labels? There are five pieces of information that are required on all domestic malt beverage labels:
1. Brand name
2. Class and type designation

3. Net contents
4. Name and address statement
5. Government Warning statement

For imported malt beverages there's an additional requirement, which is a country of origin statement.

Brand name. This is generally the most prominent name on the label. In cases where there is no such prominent name, the brewer's name satisfies this requirement so long as it appears on the front of the container. The Brand Name must appear on the front of the container.

Class and type designation. This identifies the malt beverage by consumer-recognized standards, and it must appear on the front of the container. Beer, ale, porter, stout, lager, and lager beer are examples of accepted, recognized class and type designations for those specific types of malt beverages containing 0.5 percent or more alcohol.

A malt beverage containing less than 0.5 percent alcohol may not be designated as beer, ale, porter, stout, or lager. Rather it may be labeled generally as a malt beverage or more specifically as "cereal beverage" or "near beer." Any malt beverage containing less than 0.5 percent alcohol is defined as nonalcoholic, but if it is so labeled, the statement "contains less than 0.5% alcohol by volume" must appear in direct conjunction (together) with "nonalcoholic."

"Alcohol-free" is another category of malt beverage that may not be designated with a name associated with a malt beverage over 0.5 percent alcohol. If labeled alcohol-free, the malt beverage must be completely free of even a trace of alcohol.

Another type of product in the malt beverage industry is "coolers" or specialty products. These are malt-beverage based products flavored with juices, oils, spices, commercial flavors, etc. Specialty products must be designated with a truthful and adequate statement of composition listing the major components. We look at these products on a case-by-case basis in conjunction with the approved statement of process to determine an appropriate statement of composition. Composition statements can vary tremendously from product to product, but here are three examples:

1. A beer to which raspberries have been added would be acceptably designated if it were labeled with the statement of composition "Beer With Raspberries Added."

2. For an ale flavored with a commercially prepared natural cherry flavor, it would be acceptable to state, "Ale With Natural Flavor (or Natural Cherry Flavor) Added."

3. If strawberries were added to stout during the fermentation process, "Stout Fermented With Strawberries" would be an acceptable statement of composition.

Let me emphasize that these are just examples. Statements of composition for specialty products must be viewed in conjunction with your statement of process to assure that your product is appropriately designated. To assist you when reviewing statements of process for specialty malt beverages, we suggest appropriate, adequate statements of composition.

As an aside, statements of process are required for any malt beverage that is not marketed as simply beer, ale, porter, stout, lager, or lager beer. These process statements must be filed with ATF's Regional offices, where they are then forwarded to the Product Compliance Branch for our consideration. Although your notification of approval will be sent from the Region, it is our specialists who recommend approval or disapproval of the statement. It is in our recommendation to the Region that we suggest appropriate statements of composition.

I suggest that to save time, you should submit a statement of process to the Region and simultaneously send a copy to us. That way we can begin working on your statement much sooner. Be sure to note in your transmittal that you have sent copies to both the Region and Headquarters.

Net contents. This must appear on the front of the container. For containers of seven-, eleven-, and twelve-ounces, one pint, and one quart, the net contents must appear vertically to the base of the container. Other sizes are considered odd-sized and must have the net contents displayed horizontally. This is based on an old rule that is still in effect. The rule was initiated to prevent consumer confusion between historically recognized and odd-sized containers. For example, a consumer might easily confuse a 6.5-ounce container with one that is seven ounces. There are no standards of fill for malt beverages, but because of the requirement for a prominently displayed statement of net content on odd-sized containers, a consumer can easily discern the difference.

The net content statement must state the contents in American measure. In addition, you may state the fill metrically, but metric measure cannot be used in lieu of the American measure. Be sure that the content is expressed in the required units. In other words, if the content is less than one pint, it may be stated in ounces, i.e., "7 fl. oz.," "12 fl. oz.," etc. If the container is one pint but less than a quart, the contents must be expressed in fractions of a pint, i.e., "1 1/4 pints," "1 1/2 pints," or "1 pint 9 fl. oz." The same applies to containers over one quart but less than a gallon, and so forth.

Name and address. The name and address of the brewer/bottler may appear on the front or back of the container. The name is the corporate name or any approved trade name. By address we mean simply the city and state of the brewer/bottler. Your street address may appear on the label, but it isn't required.

Government Warning statement. The newest labeling requirement for all alcohol beverages is the Government Warning Statement. As mandated by the Alcohol Beverage Labeling Act of 1988, any alcoholic beverage bottled on or after November 18, 1989, must be labeled with the prescribed warning statement. On February 14, 1990, ATF published the final rule (T.D. 294) on the warning statement. The final rule did not impact the wording of the statement but did set forth certain size, type and format requirements for the warning statement. I would like to take a moment to highlight some of the more critical elements.

The two words **Government Warning** must appear in bold print. None of the remaining statement may appear in bold print.

The final rule established a third type size requirement for the warning statement. For containers over three liters in size, the Government Warning must appear in print or type not smaller than 3 mm. For containers over eight fluid ounces, the minimum type size is 2 mm. On containers of eight fluid ounces or less, the Government Warning must be at least 1 mm. The type size requirement applies to all letters, lower as well as uppercase, in the statement.

Table 1
Type Size and Characters Per Inch on Labels

Containers over 3 liters	3 mm	12 char./in.
Containers over 8 fl. oz.	2 mm	25 char./in.
Containers 8 fl. oz. or less	1 mm	40 char./in.

The third major item was the introduction of a maximum character per inch requirement based on type size. If the warning statement appears in 1 mm type, the maximum character per inch is 40. For 2 mm type, the maximum number of characters is 25; for 3 mm type, the maximum number of characters per inch is 12. Basically everything except spaces are included when counting characters per inch.

The Government Warning may appear on the front, back or side of the container. I cannot overemphasize that the warning

Pre-Conference Tour participants look at the frosty Eisbock fermentation tanks at the Niagara Falls Brewing Company in Niagara Falls, Ontario.

statement is mandated by law and is of critical concern. Bottling without the warning statement or with a noncomplying statement could subject you to a penalty of up to $10,000 per bottling.

The brand name, class and type designation, net contents, name and address, and Government Warning statement are the five pieces of information mandatory for domestic malt beverage labels, and for imported malt beverages, the requirements are the same with the addition of a country of origin statement such as "Product of (Place)." The name and address (city and country) of the foreign brewer, preceded by "Brewed by" may be used in lieu of the "Product of (Place)" statement. Or,"Brewed in (Place)" would also be acceptable. The country of origin statement is actually a U.S. Customs requirement, but we will not issue label certificates for imported products without it. It can appear on the back or front of the container.

Thus far in my discussion of labeling requirements I have made only general references to "container." All of the labeling requirements apply to all types of malt beverage containers, most commonly cans or bottles, but I want to mention the mandatory label requirements as they relate to kegs. The requirements are the same for kegs, but the information may appear on the bung or tap cover. Usually the brand name, class and type, and brewer's name and address appear on the bung cover. (This is an instance where the brewer's name may also constitute the brand name.) Since there are space constraints, the Government Warning may have to appear on a separate label. The net contents is generally imprinted into the keg so that satisfies that requirement. When you submit label applications for kegs, affix the bung or tap cover in Part III of the application along with the Government Warning label.

The container size must be noted in Item 12 on the form, so note the contents statement imprinted in the keg. Not noting the container size in Item 12 may result in the rejection of your application if the size does not appear on the label. For the most part this only applies to kegs.

Mistakes to Avoid

There are several other common problems that slow down or stop the label approval process. One is simply not signing your application. Another is not submitting the application in duplicate, both with original signatures. Others are:

1. Not submitting original labels; that is, labels in their final form. We must see the actual can or the label that will appear on the bottle to assure that the mandatory information meets all legibility requirements.

2. Not submitting an etched bottle. If you intend to use bottles that are etched, we have to see the bottle itself and it must be filled with the labeled product. Believe me, we're not looking for free samples, again we're checking legibility.

3. Not complying with the Government Warning statement. Particularly with cans and etched bottles, we often see that the warning statement does not meet the readily legible requirements under ordinary conditions. Be keenly aware of that with your labels.

4. When you submit labels for specialty products, be sure to enclose a copy of the approved statement of process with it. We cannot process your application without it.

Those are some of the more common reasons for rejection of malt beverage label applications. I would like to suggest that to avoid other problems you call us whenever you have questions. I mentioned our "Help Desk," use it! Also, when you're in the process of developing new labels, let us work with you during the development process. Send us your proposed label, even if it's just a sketch, so we can let you know if it looks like there may be any compliance problems. It's just a matter of helping us help you.

Jerry Bowerman is chief of the Product Compliance Branch of the Bureau of Alcohol, Tobacco and Firearms headquartered in Washington, D.C. He has worked for the ATF for sixteen years. As an inspector in various posts of duty, his main job function was to oversee the operations of distilled spirit plants, breweries and tobacco manufacturers. Since 1983, he has been stationed in bureau headquarters in Washington, D.C.

Chapter 8.

DISTRIBUTING MICROBREWED BEERS

*Thomas Potter,
Brooklyn Brewing Co.*

Whether your goal is to create a 20,000-barrel microbrewery or take advantage of your brewpub's good name and good beer by selling kegs across town, you need to understand distribution. Do you care about the quality of your beer? No matter how quality-conscious you are in the brewery, beer can turn bad as a result of mishandling once it leaves the brewery. Do you care about your beer's image? Store and bar owners see your distributor's salespeople and drivers fifty times a year, but how often do they see you? When they have a question about your beer, who can they ask? Do you value the money you put into point-of-sale materials (POS)? You can produce brilliant designs for your posters, coasters and table tents, but unless your distributor puts them out, one by one, they are never seen by the consumer. Achieving decent distribution may be the single most important—but least understood—element of success for a new microbrewery.

I would like to share with you a perspective gained—sometimes painfully—by the Brooklyn Brewery in our nearly four years of distributing gourmet beers. I will discuss how to choose a distributor, how to treat him or her, how to set realistic goals in your

home market or farther away, and whether or not you should become your own distributor.

Terra Incognito for Microbrewers

Making good beer is fun. The chance to make our own beer is why most us get into the microbrewery business. Promoting beer can be fun, too. There are worse ways to make a living than conducting beer tastings and getting to know every bartender in town. As a brewer or potential brewer, you probably know that besides making beer, you are also getting into the promotion business.

Promotion is a necessity. But what may not be so clear—and what may not seem like fun—is the fact that you are inevitably getting involved in distribution.

Between your brewery and the customer is a wide, treacherous expanse called distribution. Between your JV Northwest racking room (which you already know and love), and your retailer's Perlick draft system (which you may never love but will certainly come to know!), there is a GMC truck with a distributor's name on its door. If you haven't made arrangements for that truck to come to your dock, don't bother brewing any beer. That seems obvious to me, but what is astonishing is the number of microbrewers who did not understand that, or understood it too late, or held perceptions far removed from reality.

Lessons from Brooklyn Brewery and Soho Soda

Our own experience at the Brooklyn Brewery is instructive. We now sell Brooklyn Lager through outside distributors into ten states, Germany, Japan, and England. Within New York State, we distribute our own products. In addition, we are the exclusive distributor in the New York City metropolitan region (including Westchester and Long Island) for seventy other gourmet beers. We distribute beer from, for example, Catamount, Dock Street, D.L. Geary Brewing Company, Bert Grant's Yakima Brewing Company, Massachusetts Bay Brewing Company, August Schell, Sierra Nevada, Telluride, Upper Canada, and Yuengling. But when we began business in 1988, our business was only in Brooklyn, and only with Brooklyn Lager. Our business plan indicated that we would start out self-distributing in Brooklyn with a van, warehouse, and two salespeople. When we expanded outside Brooklyn, we would appoint other distributors. When sales in Brooklyn rose to a level where we had proved that the beer was attractive commercially, we would turn over distribution there, too. That was the plan. It did not work out as we expected.

Initially, we resisted the idea of doing any of our own distribution. It is not a romantic part of the beer business, especially in New York. But we were fortunate to receive some very good advice from our famous neighbor, Sophia Collier, who founded Soho Soda and lived just up 8th Street in Brooklyn from my partner, Steve Hindy, and me. After nearly a decade of hard work, she had built Soho Soda into an $18 million company. (She would sell it to Seagram's within a year.)

She told us that the only way to truly learn distribution—to not be afraid of it, or misunderstand the process, or be intimidated by other distributors—was to do it yourself. It was not mysterious, she said, it simply took hard work. She pointed out that although Soho Soda tried many distribution arrangements in its early years, its business only became successful when it began self-distributing.

We followed Sophia Collier's advice. Although we appointed other distributors in surrounding counties, we always kept our own distributorship in Brooklyn. It was a good thing, too, because we were often disappointed by our outside distributors. In the past, we opened up a new territory and got really excited. When we introduced Brooklyn Lager, there would be 30 salespeople in the room representing 3,000 accounts. The sales manager would declare that ours was a great new product—one of the best—and that the distributor was behind it 100 percent. We would mentally perform the multiplication, and trying to be "conservative," we would assume that if each salesperson were to sell just one case each day, we would total over 600 cases each month. But then we would be disappointed when after six months, it became obvious that twenty-eight of the thirty salespeople were not selling even one case a month.

We began to wonder about these twenty-eight. Were they lazy? In a coma? Not properly motivated? We tried everything. Huge incentives per case sold. Incentives to the managers. Lower prices. Heavy promotion schedules. Then, it began to dawn on us that perhaps nothing would work. We saw the hard truth: If a distributor and its staff couldn't understand gourmet beer, nothing you could do would ever be enough. So now the question is, how do you choose the right distributor?

How to Choose a Distributor

In choosing a distributor, many factors influence the decision: personal chemistry, size, geographical reach, financial strength, and the "fit" between the distributorship and your product. Of these, one of the most powerful element is personal chemistry. If you have a chance to know the senior management or owners of a distributorship, and they are enthusiastically behind your beer, then your chances for doing well are obviously better than if your product is lost among dozens of others. Yet, as powerful as personal chemistry can be, it's also difficult to judge. At your initial meeting, the distributor can be your new best friend declaring your beer the best he or she has ever tasted. He or she may enthuse that together you will sell a 1,000 cases a month initially, and maybe more later. But enthusiasm can wane. What will happen a year later, if instead of selling 1,000 cases a month, you are only selling 50, and if there are other new products that have taken your place in his heart?

What happens if the ownership or management changes? Personal chemistry is powerful, fragile and volatile. While it can be of great help and is a legitimate factor in your decision, you also have to be careful. Love can fade.

Size is another factor in choosing a distributorship. Bigger may seem to be better. If there are more salespeople visiting more accounts on your behalf, they may sell more of your beer. But the great unknown is whether you will still get attention after several months. It is a sad fact that smaller products generally get lost in larger organizations, and this trade off will be a constant worry for you. Also, a larger organization may well have a number of other beers in direct competition with yours—perhaps imported beers or beers from American micros that have been in-house longer and are already established. How will your beer fit in? Or you might approach a larger distributor that does not have any product in your category, and then you might wonder whether the salespeople understand the fine points of selling a gourmet product. Bigger may sometimes be better, but not always.

The geographical reach of a distributorship is a concern to you. First, you need to think through the big picture in your state. In any given state, there are likely to be parallel networks of distributorships based on flagship brands. For instance, a state might have five Miller distributors, each located near a major city and covering several counties. Likewise, there might be a Bud network, Coors network, Stroh's network, and sometimes several independent distributors who work together as an informal network.

In choosing one distributor, your choice will very likely affect who else will take your beer. For instance, you may want to be with a Bud distributor in Albany but a Miller distributor in Buffalo. Or a Coors distributor in Columbus and an independent in Cincinnati. You may not, however, be able to make a "mixed marriage" of distributors work.

What you need to do is identify the most important area for you, the largest city or the one with the most potential for your beer, and decide which distributor would be your first choice in that locale. Then, you can plan how the rest of the mosaic fits together. The best solution is usually to attract an entire network, but if one Miller distributor were to take your product, and the others would not, what do you do? Your first priority is to cover well the most important area, and you may be forced to make compromises outside of that.

Another consideration is the basic advantages to doing business with fewer distributors. Each distributor you appoint requires maintenance. Billing, calls, shipping, and promotional programs all take time. In addition, if you split your sales in a given area among several distributors, each one of them is likely to sell less. Because yours is a gourmet product, you may find it spread so thin that it becomes unattractive to distributors. A distributor who covers a wider territory such as several counties or cities may have an easier time handling a gourmet beer. He can order it in sufficient quantities to ship efficiently but still keep it fresh.

The financial strength of a distributor is important for reasons both obvious and subtle. Clearly, you want to be paid. Most distributors want to pay on a net thirty- or forty-five-day basis, and you want to feel comfortable that a check really is coming. Also, a financially strong distributor has less staff turnover, better people and better morale. These attributes should be important to you. I have heard it said that sales of microbrewed beers are not affected much by sales of beers from big breweries. But on an individual level, what if your largest distributor is a Stroh's house? Your sales with him may be nicely up, but if his Stroh's sales are down, he is laying off salespeople, and his check bounces, you will certainly feel the affect.

A factor that goes beyond the objective criteria is the matter of "fit." Beer distributorships are usually based on a flagship brand, and their fortunes generally rise or fall depending on how the patron brewery is doing. There is, for example, a character to a Bud house; the distributor typically limits his products to Anheuser-Busch and a very few imported brands. He is financially successful. He is likely to be professional, and if he wants your product, he may well do an outstanding job. But be wary of forcing yourself on your local Bud distributor. Keep in mind that the salespeople for Budweiser may never have had to sell a difficult product, and are mostly in the business of taking orders and allocating shortages. (It is nice business, if you can get it!)

In a typical market, the Bud distributor may be the largest and most profitable, followed by the Miller distributor, which may also have a number of imported brands in addition to its primary Miller brands. The Miller network may also be successful, professional, and profitable, and it may offer you the additional advantage of actually wanting your beer. In most markets there are also independent distributors, and those based on declining flagship brands. In many states, the Stroh's distributorships, or those based on Heilemann products, have recently been undergoing rough times. This should not immediately disqualify them because they can still be first-rate operations, with strong imported brands. Besides, they may be most receptive to your beer, which is a real plus.

The question is, how will a particular distributor do with an unadvertised, unknown, expensive beer, which is your beer? Maybe not so well, if its main product is Colt 45 or Ballantine Ale. How will the salespeople feel about selling a twenty-two-dollar-a-case gourmet beer? You have to look beyond the ownership and the management, and make an educated guess about how the actual salesforce will feel about your product. Sometimes owner or manager attention is what counts, and the salespeople snap into line. But more often, there is inertia in an organization, and no matter what the owner thinks, the salespeople sell what sells easily. If your beer is a hard sell, it won't get sold no matter what the incentives are. So ask yourself what are the salespeople used to selling.

Consider also the type of accounts the distributor has. If on-premise draft business is important to you, make sure the distributorship has that type of business. Also keep in mind that draft accounts are hard to get, and salespeople are loath to give them up. So if the distributor you have chosen also carries Bass Ale, for example, don't expect a salesman who has been making money on Bass Ale for the last two years to suggest that a bar owner take Bass Ale off tap and try this wonderful new beer of yours.

A Hero at Home

Like any enterprise, yours likely has a combination of strengths and weaknesses, and your chances for success are based not so much on how long those lists are but on how well you adapt to them. It seems clear that microbreweries have as their great strength local or regional appeal. Local pride exists almost everywhere in the United States. One facet of this is the "local angle" phenomenon of newspapers wherein newspapers search out a local angle on topics in the news. If there's a national story on beer and yours is the local beer, then your product is the angle. Your beer gets press and develops local recognition.

Likewise, because you are local, you can lavish attention on local establishments that carry your beer. Then, the attention is not just from an ordinary salesperson, but from the owner of the brewery, or the brewmaster, or some other significant employee. No Bud distributor or Corona import agent can hire a regional manager as committed, knowledgeable or enthusiastic as you can be. In fact, if you can't attract the attention and affection of dozens of prime local accounts, then you are doing something very wrong.

A microbrewery also has the local advantage of fresher beer. Typically you are competing in your home market more against imports than other microbrewed product, and you can make the legitimate case that your beer tastes better. Even when compared to other American microbeers, in your home market you are likely to turn your beer over more quickly and remedy problems where accounts are not rotating their stocks properly. These are your primary strengths, and your local distributor will quickly grasp them. You have an attractive product for him, and he can understand that he can move enough of your product to make money on it. Whether he can move enough so that you can make money is another matter.

Lost Abroad

All of these strengths of the small brewery lose power as the epicenter of distribution widens. In your home town you are a king, in your county you are a prince, and even out in the far regions of your state, you are at least a somebody. But as you cross state lines, you can quickly become a nobody.

Consider the weaknesses of a microbrewery; typically we are not yet well organized. We are struggling to understand the traditional beer business. We don't come from the big bad beer world, and so we don't yet know what people who have sold beer for twenty-five years know about customers. Whereas a big brewery has its promotions planned a year ahead of time and provides POS and promotional material, a small brewer is lucky if he or she remembers two weeks before the 4th of July that the holiday is coming. A small brewer probably doesn't have the money to advertise and must depend instead on word-of-mouth advertising. The small brewer has less volume over which to amortize overhead—which has obvious consequences. You may spend more for POS and promotion on a per case basis than Budweiser ever dreamed of, and yet it may still add up to only a paltry few thousand dollars a month. A mere drop in a bucket in a distributor's eyes.

Look at your strengths, look at your weaknesses, and you can see why most small breweries sell most of their beer close to home. How much is most? Almost all. In my experience, public appearances are deceiving. We read in *The New Brewer* about microbreweries opening up distribution out-of-state and exporting to new countries because every brewery is working hard to build excitement for its brand. But by and large, most micros sell the vast majority of their beer in their local market. What does "local market" mean? Usually it is a metropolitan area. Sometimes it might be a whole state. In certain instances, it might be parts of two or three states. But whatever or however we define the local nest, I believe most breweries sell between 75 and 95 percent of their beer close to home. I think it is a very rare small brewery that sells as much as a 25 percent outside its home market.

What does this mean? Say we are imagining a prototypical 5,000-barrel microbrewery, now in it's fifth year, succeeding locally. In addition, it sells to twenty distributors in ten other states. Let's say it sells 80 percent of its beer locally. That means 1,000 barrels are sold outside the home market, the equivalent of about 1,000 cases a month. Among twenty distributors, that is fifty cases a month. One pallet a month. Not a big number.

I have seen many business plans for hopeful micros. They often plan on selling 1,000 cases a month in surrounding states. The numbers seem to add up quickly. By the time expansion steamrolls through all fifty states, you have a Business Plan Beer Baron. But it won't be so easy. There are comparatively few microbeers that sell more than 100 cases a month in a state far from home. There may be one or two states where the beer does better than average, and there are others where it does less. Look at the list of the top twenty micros—I can assure you that beyond Boston Beer Company, The Anchor Brewing Company, Sierra Nevada, and one or two others, not even the familiar brands sell much more than 100 cases a month in any state far from home.

Realistic Goals

This needn't discourage you. You can do several things to improve your performance and take other actions to adapt, but the key is to be realistic. If you expect to sell fifty cases a month to an out-of-town distributor, you need to provide case cards, shelf talkers, some free beer for sampling, and a basic sales sheet for salespeople to hand out. You want to introduce the beer at a sales meeting, and perhaps spend days with some of the salespeople or managers. Offer a competitive price, preferably a "delivered" price, so the distributor doesn't have to source and price shipping. At this level, you are a minor brand. The distributor will not drop his other affairs to greet you at the door, but nevertheless you are a viable brand. The distributor can buy two pallets of your beer at a time and hope the brand grows. Whether or not it does will be up to you. If you would like to sell more than 100 cases a month, or if you want to sell draft, you may need to increase your level of support. Consider having a sales manager visit the market a few days each month. (As a rough guess, each 100 cases may take one day a month.) This representative should visit accounts, not just the distributor. You may also have to offer price support for volume customers, chain store sales, and periodic promotions. Your distributor may co-op many costs, but he will look to you for significant support.

If your goal is to sell 1,000 cases a month or more, you are

Beer is being brewed during the Pre-Conference Tour at the Conners Brewery in St. Catharines, Ontario.

aiming for rarified company. Count on a full-time salesperson and heavy POS support. Beyond 2,000 cases, consider radio or print advertising. More than that, and you don't need my advice.

The Wine House Alternative

In many states where it is legal, wine and liquor distributors are now seeking out microbeers for the first time. As their traditional product sales levels slump, the impressive recent growth of micros is a powerful lure to them. They are used to selling low-volume, high-margin, unadvertised "story" products. In addition, their salespeople are typically better educated, more polished, and more comfortable with upscale accounts than salespeople from beer distributors. Too often, beer salespeople are used to selling primarily on price and deals. Wine salespeople expect to sell on quality. In this regard they are well suited to selling microbeers.

Consider, however, if certain potential disadvantages apply: Will the wine distributor handle draft? (Do you want and expect to support draft sales?) Does it call on chain stores? (Can you get chain store authorizations?) Does it have customer discount and sales commission structures that suit volume beer sales? (Will you be achieving volume sales levels?) If you can live with or overcome the disadvantages, the wine house alternative might be attractive. It requires less maintenance at low- to modest-sales levels. Choosing a wine house may limit your upside potential somewhat, but most micros overrate their upside potential in out of town markets anyway.

Should You Self-Distribute?

The answer to the question is, yes, in your home market. There, the ripe cherry accounts are most numerous, and easiest to reach. The experience you gain will be priceless. If it is legal in your state, it is probably worth your effort. The margins will be high enough to overcome the inevitable mistakes you will make while learning on the fly. You can always give distribution to someone else later if your product is a success, and it is more likely to become a success if you do it yourself first.

Outside your immediate home market, maybe self-distribution isn't the answer. A one-product distributorship faces increasing economic obstacles the farther from home it gets.Taking on complementary products can extend your range, but be prepared for a long, hard road. At that point, you must become a professional quality distributor as well as a professional quality brewer. There is no better guarantee of attention than extending your own direct purview, but be prepared with some fundamental changes in outlook. You must calculate whether or not you have the resources and inclination to jump into that ring. Your competitors as a direct distributor will be of a different character than your mostly collegial competitors as a small brewer.

Table 1
Truck Costs

	$/Month	Case Capacity	Maximum Cases/Month	Average Cases/Month	$/Case
Van	900	90	1890	945	1.05
High Cube	1200	150	3150	1575	.76
Light Truck	1500	250	5250	2625	.57
Heavy Truck	2000	600	12600	6300	.31

An Economic Primer

Whether you distribute your own beer or appoint someone else, you should understand the basic economics involved. Although the details are endlessly complicated, the principles are straightforward. A distributor buys beer and sells it. From its margin, it pays for trucks, drivers, salespeople, a warehouse, an administrative staff, and hopefully has something left over.

Truck costs vary widely from region to region. The elements include leasing or financing costs, insurance, gas, maintenance, tickets, licensing, and registration. Each geographic area has unique circumstances that bear on costs. A rural area may have higher gas costs. An urban area likely has higher insurance costs. Overall, urban areas may be somewhat higher than rural areas. But in general, the costs shown are fairly typical, and the relationship between the costs of different kinds of trucks holds steady everywhere.

Of more interest than the raw cost of the truck is what the cost per case is—how efficient the truck can be in delivering beer. A van is clearly the least efficient, although for a small operation it is also the easiest to use. The van's capacity is determined by weight, not volume, and a typical heavy-duty van can only carry about ninety cases of longnecks. If you aren't worried about weight, you might be able to load as many as 130 or 140 cases, but you might also break the axles on the first pothole.

At ninety cases, a twenty-one-day month would indicate a maximum delivery capability of 1,890 cases. However, you are unlikely—with a van, or any other truck—to reach this maximum. There are dozens of reasons why the theoretical maximum capacity is unreachable. Every day there will be orders refused, empties to be picked up, and stops that suddenly can't pay. There will be some days when the driver is sick, or the truck is down for maintenance. After one booming week, business mysteriously dwindles the next.

Keep in mind, too, that there are other constraints in the real world of distributing. Stops per day is one. In the heart of Manhattan, where we at the Brooklyn Brewery deliver to 150 chain stores in a five-mile radius, we can deliver to as many as twenty-five stops a day. But that number can drop by half if the driver also has to put up merchandising displays, take back empties, wait for a check, wait for an assistant manager's approval, or rearrange a shelf that the Coors driver rearranged an hour earlier. Human lifting limits are another constraint. Each case of longnecks weighs about thirty-five pounds. If the deliveries are for full pallets, a forklift does the work. Most sales, though, are handtrucked in. It is heavy work, especially if you are bouncing the handtruck down steps to a basement. I recall one otherwise sound business plan that projected delivering an average of 200 cases a day out of a van, loading up twice a day. It is physically impossible. Vans not only unload by hand, but also are loaded by hand. Even Godzilla on steroids would burn out on that regimen.

The challenge for the distributor is to work toward maximum efficiency, but it is a rare distributor who can consistently achieve a lot more than half of capacity. In the hotel business, 90 percent occupancy is considered as high as is desirable; beyond that, the hotel can't perform regular maintenance. In the distribution business, the practical maximum is probably closer to 50 than 90 percent.

Table 2
Salary Costs Per Month

	Driver	Helper	Sales 1	Sales 2	Total
Van (A)	$2,000				$2,000
Van (B)	2,000		2,000		4,000
High Cube	2,000		2,000		4,000
Light Truck	2,000		2,000		4,000
Heavy Truck (C)	2,500		2,000		4,500
Heavy Truck (D)	2,500	1,000	2,000	2,000	7,500

Salary costs, of course, vary enormously depending on general labor costs for a market. Assumed here are total costs for a driver without a heavy truck license of about $20,00 a year, with benefits of about $4,000 a year—total costs of $2,000 a month. A driver with a heavier class license is likely to demand a higher salary, and if unionized even higher still. Two scenarios are shown in Table 2 for vans and for heavy trucks. For the vans scenario "A," the driver is also the salesperson. He or she is making calls, trying to sell beer to each stop, and then immediately delivering beer right off his truck. Under scenario "B," the van driver is augmented by a full-time salesperson, and it is assumed that the salesperson will place orders that the driver delivers and merchandises the next day. If a driver also has to sell beer, he or she is likely to sell less than the projected average cases per month. If he is supported by a full-time salesperson, the team may sell more than the projected average cases per month. The two scenarios for heavy trucks are "C," a driver with one salesperson and "D," a driver accompanied by a helper, likely to be unskilled labor, delivering for two salespeople. It is fairly typical for a medium to large distributor to have roughly a 2:1 ratio of salespeople to drivers. Each salesperson might be

Table 3
Selling & Delivery Costs

	Truck	Salary	Total	Average Cases	$/Case
Van (A)	$900	$2,000	$2,900	$700	4.14
Van (B)	900	4,000	4,900	1250	3.92
High Cube	1200	4,000	5,200	1575	3.30
Light Truck	1500	4,000	5,500	2625	2.04
Heavy Truck(C)	2000	4,500	6,500	4000	1.62
Heavy Truck (D)	2000	7,500	9,500	7000	1.35

responsible for up to 150 accounts He would see prime accounts weekly, or even bi-weekly, and minor accounts every two or three weeks.

The growing efficency of larger trucks is obvious. The least efficient case is a van with driver sales, the most efficent case is a heavy truck with full sales support and a helper on board. Of course, these efficiencies are only captured if the heavier vehicles are needed. Delivering fifty cases a day out of a heavy truck is clearly more expensive than delivering out of a van. An ideal day from a distributor's point of view is dropping fifty-case pallets to ten forklift-wielding cash customers who ordered two days in advance. For that, a heavy truck is perfect. But on days when ten stops are ordering five cases each, that heavy truck takes on a certain hollow sound.

In addition to truck, driver and sales costs, a distributor has overhead costs: a warehouse, offices, forklifts, computers, several administrative staffers, possibly some sales managers, and a top manager or two. How much does this add up to? Much depends on size, with considerable scale efficiencies possible. A small distributor might need to cover $1.50 per case in general and administrative overhead. A larger distributor might drive this price down to $0.50 per case, or less. Taken all in all, then, a very large distributor might be able to deliver cases at an average price of as little as $1.50 per case for bottles. Most distributors, though, will be closer to $2.00 per case. Smaller distributors or those without a big volume brand, will pay $3.00 per case or more.

Average costs per case, however, can be somewhat misleading. A distributor thinks about incremental costs, not average costs. Thus, if a truck is leaving every day half full, and your beer can add ten cases a day to it, what is the incremental cost of delivering those 200 cases per month? If they are going to stops that would have been made anyway, the answer is, very little. That is why your cases matter. They may represent less than one percent of sales to a distributor, but most distributors operate within a few percentage points of breakeven. Your beer, along with a few others, might mean the difference between profit and loss in a given month.

Pricing

How much will a distributor pay for your beer? Most distributors work backwards. They may tell you, for instance, that in their market the leading micro is Sierra Nevada (or Brooklyn Lager or Dock Street), and that it wholesales at a front line price of $20 per case, discounted back to an average price of $18 per case. That allows retailers to meet a price point of $5.99 per six-pack at a 25 percent margin. The distributor, too, wants a 25 percent margin. That indicates a tax-paid freight-in price to him of $13.50. Can you meet it?

Perhaps not. You might point out that the wholesaler and retailer work on much more "reasonable" margins for their other products, which is likely true. However, those products are also likely to be much easier to sell and deliver and may sell through more quickly. At the retail level, stores that work on 10 percent or less for Budweiser try to make up the difference on beers like yours. You will not change too many minds about pricing, until you can deliver a track record on volume.

At our company, we have wholesale micro pricing in three ranges. At the $18 per case level is Brooklyn Lager and Brooklyn Brown. At the $20 to 22 per case level are most others, which come to us at about $15 to16 per case delivered (including state and city taxes). Within each of these categories, pricing does matter. If a buyer is choosing between Anchor and Sierra, or between Brooklyn and Sam Adams, pricing counts. A $5.99 six-pack can sell nearly twice as much as a $6.99 six-pack. So consider which of three categories you wish to compete in:

Table 4
Micro Market Categories

	Market Leader	Upscale Placements	Specialty Placements
1. Typical Wholesale	$16 - $19 Reg. Post-offs	$20 -$22 Some Post-offs	$23 + Some Post-offs
2. Chain Stores	Most	Some	None
3. Draft Accts.	Most	Some	None
4. Support	Heavy POS Fulltime mgr. Schedules promos Local PR and/or Ads	POS Pt-time mgr. Limited promos	POS
Case Sales/Mo. Keg sales/Mo.	500 + 25 +	50-500 Up to 25	Up to 50 0

Table 5
Micro Pricing

	Distributor	Wholesale	Retail
Market Leader			
25% Margins	$13.50	$18	$5.99
20% Post-off	12.50	16	4.99
Upscale Placements			
25% Margins	$15.75	$21	$6.99
20% Post-offs	14.75	19	5.99
Specialty Placements			
25% Margins	$18	$24	$7.99
20% Post-offs	17	22	6.99

- Chance for category market leadership, with heavy support, volume pricing, universal chain sales, and wide draft placements.
- Upscale placements, chance at some chain stores and prestige draft accounts, or
- Specialty placements, in accounts that look for a variety of beers or which have some theme connection to your brewery. Then look at the competition's pricing, and work backwards.

Summary

Distribution is easiest and most profitable close to a microbrewery's home market. Attracting a local distributor to carry the beer will not be difficult. Some consideration, however, should be given to self-distribution. The margins may be high enough to compensate for early mistakes, and the learning process is invaluable. Choosing a distributor is a matter of setting realistic sales goals, judging honestly the strengths and weaknesses of your own operation and those of the potential distributors', and focusing on priorities. Outside the home market, more effort will be required to sell each case. Recognizing this, a brewery must decide in which sales category it wishes to compete and whether or not it can provide the concurrent level of pricing and sales support necessary.

Thomas Potter is co-founder and C.E.O. of the Brooklyn Brewery, which in 1990, began a distribution division to act as master distributor in metro New York for its own beers and seventy gourmet beers from around the world. The company's products are available in 10 states, Japan, Germany, and England.

Chapter 9.

BREWPUB DESIGN EFFICIENCY

Steve Fried,
McGuire's Irish Pub and Brewery

Eight years ago, when I was in the U.S. Navy and stationed in Japan, I toured the Suntory Brewery near Tokyo. It was the most incredibly huge and sophisticated brewery I had ever seen. But what impressed me most was the lack of people. On the tour, I saw only two workers—one guy sitting alone behind a computer console and another operating a forklift during a canning operation. My impression of the brewery was that it had total operational efficiency. Of course, the modern, high-tech brewery, whether here or in Japan, comes with a terrific price tag, but that is okay when the cost is spread out over millions of barrels of beer produced annually. But what does a brewpub have in common with a huge, modern brewery? Not a whole lot, except that both are in the business of producing and selling beer for profit, and therefore production efficiency makes a very important contribution to the bottom line.

The topic of my presentation is design efficiency in the restaurant/brewery, and I would like to emphasize the word *design* because that is where efficiency begins. It is too late to do much after you have built a million-dollar brewery and then discover that

you are losing money on every glass of beer you sell. Somewhere in the planning process the question needs to be asked, "What is the mission of a restaurant brewery?" My answer is, the mission of the restaurant/brewery is threefold:
- Make good beer
- Satisfy demand
- Minimize fixed and variable production costs.

Make Good Beer

The importance of "good" beer is obvious to all of us, but what is it? We as producers don't make that determination. Instead, it is the customer who plunks his empty glass on the bar and says, "Gimme another." Or "Bartender, there's a hole in the bottom of my glass!" Ultimately, your brewpub patron defines whether or not a beer is "good" by his purchase. My experience at McGuire's Irish Pub is that style does not mean or matter much for the simple reason that the public doesn't know much about style. In over two years, only a handful of people have inquired whether we have a lager. Yet, they didn't turn down our ale in favor of a Bud. An award-winning recipe not withstanding, how does your beer taste to "Joe Six-Pack?" You might be brewing a Russian Imperial Lambic Stout that makes beer writer Michael Jackson do back flips in the hall, but if it doesn't sell in your local market, it isn't good beer and it isn't worth the trouble or the space in your brewery.

Satisfy Demand

If your beer is good, it will create demand, which is why you have to design a system to meet present and future demand. But you don't want too much excess capacity because that would cost money. At McGuire's, we have a seven-barrel brewhouse—a size I feel is suitable and efficient in a system capable of producing up to 2,000 barrels annually at the rate of one brew every day. The tanks are good space savers, yet they are large enough for easy cleaning by hand from the inside.

Minimize Fixed and Variable Production Costs

The costs, both fixed and variable, in producing beer can be listed as follows:
1. Cost of capital-debt/equity financing
2. Labor
3. Raw material
4. Taxes
5. Repairs and maintenance
6. Utilities
7. Supplies
8. Administration and miscellaneous

In designing a brewery, the costs of capital and labor are crucial. If you make a mistake in designing for these, you will likely be stuck with it, and it could even doom your project. There is a relationship between capital and labor that I will demonstrate by being absurd. Let's say that you were to miniaturize the design of a large, modern brewery like Suntory to produce 1,000 barrels of beer annually for your restaurant. It might cost $5 million, but hey, you figure there will be no labor cost. The only problem is, the yearly interest on the loan will be $500,000 dollars or $500 per barrel. Over a dollar per glass! But what about the opposite situation? Say you were to build a no-cost brewery by having all the local homebrewers in your area lend you their brewing equipment and then make your beer for the wage of $10 per hour. Because it would take these guys at least four man-hours to make a five-gallon batch of beer, your labor cost would be $250 per barrel, and that would be with three brewers working in your restaurant twenty-four hours a day. The optimum labor and capital mix is capacity dependent.

Applied Efficiency

I would like to examine how these concepts of efficiency have been applied in McGuire's Irish Pub. McGuire's started out as a small neighborhood bar in 1977 and has expanded and developed to become one of the top 100 restaurants in Florida according to *Florida Trend* magazine. When brewpubs were legalized in Florida in 1987, McGuire Martin began investigating the feasibility of adding a brewery to his already successful restaurant. Though the project took longer that expected, our first keg was tapped in March 1989. and I have been brewing like mad ever since.

If you were to apply conventional wisdom to McGuire's, our brewery should have been a failure. McGuire Martin—who had no background knowledge in brewing operations—hired his heating-and-air-conditioning contractor—who had no experience in building brewing equipment—to build a brewery. Then he hired me, a local homebrewer, who had no experience brewing in a commercial scenario, to brew his beer. How could the brewery possibly succeed? But if you combine the determination and financial resources of the owner, the skill of the builder, the existing market for the beer, and the design and training assistance of a competent consultant, it can be done. (See Table 1.) As for myself, I can take no credit for the design of this system. I was hired and trained to operate it, and that is all I do.

In order to construct a brewery, McGuire had to sacrifice a dining room—a source of income. By necessity, the entire brewery had to fit into a space of 270 square feet. We installed a seven-barrel infusion mash system utilizing used stainless dairy tanks and other salvage or locally fabricated equipment. The brewery is outfitted with a mash lauter tun, brewkettle, four open fermenters, and a bright beer tank. A steam boiler and glycol chiller were put on the

Table 1
Ingredients for Success

Good Design:	Simplicity
	Efficiency
	Low Cost
Good People:	Owner
	Consultant
	Fabricator
	Brewer

Pub Brewer Qualifications

Desire:	Burning desire to make beer
Dedication:	To the art and science of making good beer
Willingness:	To work long and hard at unpleasant tasks
Mental Ability:	To be innovative, resourceful and trainable
Physical Ability:	To bend, lift, scrub, and persevere

roof. The total cost of installation was approximately $100,000. This was for a brewery with an annual capacity of just under 1,000 barrels. For the calendar year 1990, we produced 805 barrels or an average of thirty-one kegs per week. All of the beer we produce is sold and consumed on-premise in accordance with Florida law. A batch is ready to keg and drink in eleven to fourteen days. We make four kinds of ale: a light, red, porter, and stout.

To get back to my discussion of capital and labor costs, the annual interest on the loan taken to build the brewery is $12,000 or $15 per each barrel produced in 1990. In 1990, the average labor cost for myself, my substitute brewer, and my brass polisher was $430 per week or $28 per barrel. I estimate that about 3.5 man-hours went into each barrel of McGuire's Irish Ale. This compares to one-fifth of a man-hour or twelve man-minutes per barrel in a large brewery. The cost of labor in a brewpub is inherently high, even if it is automated, and a high-tech brewery probably requires a brewer commanding a high-tech salary. The brewery at McGuire's is a very manual system that is very labor intensive. I keg all the beer we produce and hand-truck the kegs myself through the restaurant to the beer coolers. I have a wheelbarrow to move spent grain and pumps to move liquids. Why do I do all this hard work?

Table 2
1990 Production Costs

1. Cost of Capital	$ 12,000
2. Labor	22,267
3. Raw Materials	19,932
4. Taxes	17,545
5. Maintenance and Repairs	2,500*
6. Utilities	2,800*
7. Supplies	5,032
8. Administration and Misc.	<u>6,324*</u>
	$ 88,400

* estimates

McGuire's Irish Ale

Sales =	$401,029
Expenses =	88,400
Gross Margin	$312,629
Cost of Goods = 22%	

Cost per barrel

Capital	$15
Labor	28
Malt and Hops	25
Taxes	22
Other Expenses	20
(Maintenance, utilities, supplies, etc.)	
	$110 per barrel
	$ 55 per keg

Besides the fact that I love it and need the exercise, it is for very practical, economic reasons.

In a low-volume operation such as a brewpub, the incremental cost of brewing equipment designed to reduce labor cost is often much greater than the labor cost saved. For example, why spend a fortune on expensive, hard stainless piping to move the product when it only takes a few minutes of time to hook up and breakdown hoses? Conversely, a large brewery emphasizes capital over labor costs to be efficient. It is cheaper and better, for example, to install a CIP system than to hire 100 grunts to scrub tanks all day by hand. So when you are thinking about buying brewery equipment, ask yourself, is this a necessary expense to fulfill the brewery's mission: to make good beer in ample supply with the minimum production cost to yield maximum profit. (See Table 2.)

Another important consideration for the restaurant operator is the limited space available for the brewery. In the case of McGuire's, space dictated much of the design. For example, our equipment manufacturer had to build a heat exchanger only five inches wide because it had to fit between a fermenter and the sink. There was only room for one bright beer tank, so serving tanks were out of the question. You might wonder why we didn't use malt extract to save space. Our consultant felt all-grain brewing was worth the effort and assured me I could handle it even though I had never made a decent batch of it in my life.

I don't want to get involved in the debate over the advantages and disadvantages of all-grain and extract brewing other than to say that with the right equipment all-grain is easy. I have had no problems of any significance. My personal viewpoint is that I feel prouder as a brewer to be able to say I make my beer from scratch. Briess Malting has prepared some excellent papers on the pros and cons of extract vs. grain. At McGuire's we use preground grain from Briess and find it very suitable. The extra cost of preground

is justified over the capital, maintenance and space requirements of a mill.
 At McGuire's we don't mess around with expensive pneumatic or mechanical grain elevators. We use the old, reliable, pack-mule system to the hopper: me. I carry the grain up and over the roof, one bag at a time. It keeps me busy while I am heating up water. Our spent grain removal system is a hoe, wheelbarrow and a dozen plastic bags.
 Everyone has heard of CIP. Our system is called "CBS," cleaning by Steve. It consists of a five-gallon pickle bucket, which I sit on, two brushes, a paint scraper, some detergent, and an incredible tool I call the "hand-activated residue removal device" or HARRD. Others call it a stainless steel scrub pad.
 Our equipment manufacturer also built us a kegwasher for our Hoff-Stevens kegs. It has a rinse trough, hot caustic solution wash and another rinse. It cost $1,000. Our plate-and-frame filter was salvaged from a winery, and we had its legs shortened because the only place we could put it blocked the view of the brewkettle. I use 5 micron cellulose filters and get sparkling clear beer. It takes me about two hours to set up the filter, sterilize it with hot water, filter a 200-gallon batch, and break the filter down.
 My lab consists of a hydrometer, thermometer, Zahm and Nagel carbon dioxide volume tester, and the most important tool of all—a tasting glass. I don't plate, culture or wash the yeast. I just scrape two gallons of yeast slurry off the bottom of my primary fermenter and put it in the cooler for a later day. I have used the same batch for ale yeast for over two years and 300 generations.
 Now that you are all appropriately horrified, I would like to make a philosophical observation. Yeast are not very smart. They have an I.Q. of zero. Yeast do what they do as they have for millions of years. The sophistication of the brewery does not impress them. Nor do they appreciate the title and background of the brewmaster.

But given the right conditions yeast do what we expect them to. I am not suggesting that lab work and modern yeast techniques have no value; they are certainly justified in a microbrewery that bottles its beer. But for a brewpub using a good strain of ale yeast and serving cold, fresh beer from well-designed and competently operated equipment, I don't see the need for them. Another advantage of an active, hardy ale yeast strain is that it produces finished beer, ready to serve in less than two weeks. Ales require half the fermentation and storage space required by lager systems, which in a brewpub translated into more space for dining tables. Ales also require less capital investment than lagers do and less utility cost.

So for you future brewpub owners on a tight budget, concentrate your design on simplicity, efficiency and low cost without compromising quality. Get a good consultant, a good fabricator, and an eager beaver for a brewer.

Steve Fried has been brewing beer at McGuire's Irish Pub in Pensacola, Florida, since the installation of the brewery in 1989. For the ten years prior, he was a dedicated extract homebrewer. He holds an M.B.A. from the University of West Florida. He prefers to be known as a hardworking S.O.B. (Student of Brewing).

Chapter 10.

INDUSTRY OVERVIEW

*David Edgar,
Institute for Brewing Studies*

Part of what microbreweries and brewpubs have accomplished during their brief history is the reeducation of American beer consumers. In many a liquor store, beer store, or grocery, the range of possible choices of beers is as follows:

- Beer
- Light beer
- Malt liquor
- Dry beer
- Dark beer

- Ale
- Cream ale
- Imported beer
- Nonalcoholic beer

Thanks to this new generation of small craft brewers, however, today's beer drinkers are learning about many other styles of traditional brewing, adding a lot of new words to their beer vocabulary:

- Pale ale
- India pale ale
- Bitter
- Amber ale
- Brown ale
- Mild ale

- Doppelbock
- Vienna
- Oktoberfest
- Munich-style
- Pilsener
- Dortmunder

- Strong ale
- Porter
- Stout
- Imperial stout
- Scotch ale
- Barley wine
- Trappist ale
- Lambic-style
- Bock

- Alt
- Steam beer
- Wheat beer
- Weisse
- Hefe-Weizen
- Fruit beer
- Herb beer
- Spiced beer
- Smoked beer

Besides offering stylistic variety, microbrewed beers generally also adhere to the philosophy of all-malt brewing. While the most popular national brands commonly utilize adjuncts such as rice and corn, which contribute to a lighter-flavored, lighter-bodied product, almost all microbrewers are brewing all-malt beers. While the light beer category has grown tremendously in recent months, this has been occurring simultaneously with a growth in the popularity of fuller-flavored beers.

I will offer a few definitions. A *microbrewery* is a brewery that produces no more than 15,000 barrels of beer annually. A *brewpub* is a combination restaurant and brewery that sells the majority of its beer on-premise. A *contract brewing company* is a company that develops and markets a brand of beer yet uses a brewery it does not own to manufacture the brand. As with microbreweries, beers from contract brewing companies typically are all-malt products and are positioned as "microbrews."

There are also combinations, however. Many microbreweries recently have added restaurants; many brewpubs have increased brewing capacity, added bottling lines, and begun aggressively pursuing off-premise accounts. Also, there are many predominantly draft-oriented brewpubs and microbreweries that have products brewed under contract at other facilities, which enables them to offer bottled product on a wider scale.

Each year the Institute for Brewing Studies asks every microbrewery, brewpub and contract brewing company in North America to answer forty different questions about their operations. The following charts show the results, representing—as best can be determined—industry-wide averages. The information is presented with separate figures for each of the five segments of the industry: U.S. brewpubs, Canadian brewpubs, U.S. microbreweries, Canadian microbreweries, and contract brewing companies. The numbers in parentheses indicate the number of responses given, where applicable.

The most common types of companies are closely held corporations and limited partnerships. Only a few are publicly held. (See Table 1.)

Last year was the first time we surveyed breweries on how much they pay their employees. We did not get an overwhelming number of responses to these questions, therefore please do not regard the amounts shown on the charts as true industry averages. Instead they are examples of the salaries some companies are paying. (See Table 2.)

In examining the openings of microbreweries and brewpubs, the most dramatic growth for U.S. microbreweries occurred during the last three years. During each of the years from 1988 to 1990, an average of more than sixteen microbreweries and fifty-five brewpubs have opened nationwide in the U.S. (See Table 3.)

Craft brewing in Canada followed a consistent pattern of growth for the four years prior to 1990, with an average of eight microbreweries and ten brewpubs opening per year from 1986 through 1989. However, in 1990, this trend proved short lived, as only one microbrewery and three brewpubs opened in Canada.

Currently, the number of small breweries in operation is eighty-nine microbreweries and 150 brewpubs in the U.S. and twenty-four microbreweries and forty-four brewpubs in Canada.

See Table 4 for averages for total production and total capacity of microbreweries and brewpubs in the U.S. and Canada.

The chart on taxable production shows the annual growth in production of the entire industry. (See Table 5.) The combined total production of U.S. micros and brewpubs grew by an average of 40 percent per year during the three-year period of 1988 through 1990. The total production of U.S. brewpubs in 1990 (based on 86 percent reporting), was up 81 percent over total production in 1989 (based on 82 percent reporting). The total production of U.S. microbreweries during 1990 (based on 87 percent reporting) increased by 45 percent over 1989 figures (based on 85 percent reporting).

Canada's combined total production of microbreweries and brewpubs grew by an average of more than 22 percent per year during 1989 and 1990.

Between June 1990 and June 1991, eight microbreweries in Ontario closed. Why? One possible explanation is that after the novelty of microbreweries wore off and as the local economy worsened, consumers became less tolerant of idiosyncracies in microbrewed beers and more demanding of quality and consistency. Ontario breweries that were making consistent, quality beer but still went under generally suffered from undercapitalization and/or management problems. The good news is that all remaining Ontario microbreweries are brewing at capacity.

Recently I added up the total number of microbrewery and brewpub openings in the U.S. and Canada between 1977 and mid-1991 and compared it with the total number of closings, to determine the failure rate as shown. (See Table 6.)

The craft brewing industry as a whole has matured since the first microbrewery opened in 1977 and the first brewpub opened in 1983. Trends can now be observed from the industry's brief history and general statements can be made about the nature of microbreweries, brewpubs and contract brewing companies.

Table 1
Type of Company

U.S. Brewpubs	(80)
Closely Held Corporation	49
Limited Partnership	15
General Partnership	8
Sole Proprietor	7
Publicly Held Corporation	1
Canadian Brewpubs	(13)
Closely Held Corporation	8
Sole Proprietor	3
Limited Partnership	2
U.S. Microbreweries	(25)
Limited Partnership	8
Sole Proprietor	7
Closely Held Corporation	4
Publicly Held Corporation	4
General Partnership	2
Canadian Microbreweries	(8)
Limited Partnership	6
Closely Held Corporation	1
Publicly Held Corporation	1
Contract Brewing Companies	(28)
Closely Held Corporation	23
Limited Partnership	4
General Partnership	1

Table 2
Employee Salaries

U.S. Brewpubs		**U.S. Microbreweries**	
Avg. No. of Brewery Employees	(78) 2.5	Avg. No. of Brewery Employees	(63) 5.0
Avg. Weekly Hours Worked	(72) 40.3	Avg. Weekly Hours Worked	(54) 43.1
Avg. Weekly Earnings	(44) $376	Avg. Weekly Earnings	(29) $404
Avg. Estimated Wage	$9.33/hr	Avg. Estimated Wage	$9.37/hr
Avg. No. of Admin. Employees	(64) 2.0	Avg. No. of Admin. Employees	(52) 1.9
Avg. Weekly Hours Worked	(56) 35.7	Avg. Weekly Hours Worked	(46) 38.3
Avg. Weekly Earnings	(34) $363	Avg. Weekly Earnings	(22) $424
Avg. Estimated Wage	$10.17/hr	Avg. Estimated Wage	$11.07/hr

Canadian Brewpubs		**Canadian Microbreweries**	
Avg. No. of Brewery Employees	(14) 1.7	Avg. No. of Brewery Employees	(17) 10.1
Avg. Weekly Hours Worked	(14) 34.7	Avg. Weekly Hours Worked	(17) 47.0
Avg. Weekly Earnings	(8) $409 Can.	Avg. Weekly Earnings	(11) $403 Can.
Avg. Estimated Wage	$11.78 Can/hr	Avg. Estimated Wage	$8.57 Can/hr
Avg. No. of Admin. Employees	(12) 1.9	Avg. No. of Admin. Employees	(17) 5.6
Avg. Weekly Hours Worked	(10) 25.5	Avg. Weekly Hours Worked	(17) 40.6
Avg. Weekly Earnings	(8) $447 Can.	Avg. Weekly Earnings	(10) $418 Can.
Avg. Estimated Wage	$17.53 Can/hr	Avg. Estimated Wage	$10.30 Can/hr

Table 3

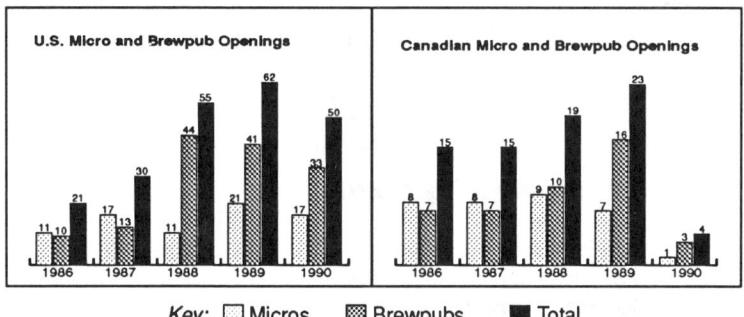

Key: Micros Brewpubs Total

Table 4
Average Estimated 1990 Total Output

U.S. Brewpubs (Bry. open full year)	(58)	949
Canadian Brewpubs (Bry. open full year)	(8)	892
U.S. Microbreweries (Bry. open full year)	(50)	3,490
Canadian Microbreweries (Bry. open full year)	(16)	6,786

Average Annual Production Capacity

U.S. Brewpubs	(80)	1,314 bbl
Canadian Brewpubs	(13)	2,242 hl
U.S. Microbreweries	(65)	4,934 bbl
Canadian Microbreweries	(18)	10,944 hl

Table 5

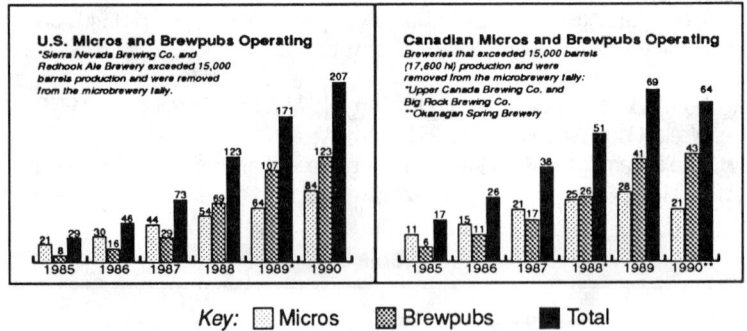

Key: ☐ Micros ▨ Brewpubs ■ Total

Table 6
Failure Rate

(Total Opened vs. Total Closed)

U.S. Brewpubs:	1 in 8
Can. Brewpubs:	1 in 5
U.S. Microbreweries:	1 in 4
Can. Microbreweries:	1 in 2

Table 7
Package Distribution

U.S. Brewpubs
Avg. % Beer Sold...
  in Bottles   (93) 3%
  in Draft   (93) 97%

U.S. Microbreweries
Avg. % Beer Sold...
  in Bottles   (75) 44%
  in Draft   (75) 56%

Canadian Brewpubs
Avg. % Beer Sold...
  in Bottles   (24) 2%
  in Draft   (24) 98%

Canadian Microbreweries
Avg. % Beer Sold...
  in Bottles   (18) 56%
  in Draft   (18) 44%

Contract Brewing Companies
Avg. % Beer Sold...
  in Bottles   (27) 79%
  in Draft   (27) 16%
  in Other   (27) 5%

Table 8
Sales Distribution: geographical

U.S. Brewpubs
Avg. Percent Sales that are . . .
 Self-distributed (45) 85%
 Distributor (45) 13%
Avg. No. of Distributors (47) 1.4
Avg. Percent Sales that are . . .
 In-state (71) 93%
 Out-of-state (71) 7%
 In-state Local (68) 94%

Canadian Brewpubs
Avg. Percent Sales that are . . .
 Self-distributed (4) 100%
Avg. Percent Sales that are . . .
 In-state (14) 100%
 In-state Local (16) 100%

Canadian Microbreweries
Avg. Percent Sales that are . . .
 Self-distributed (17) 71%
 Distributor (17) 23%
Avg. No. of Distributors (14) 2.5
Avg. Percent Sales that are . . .
 In-state (17) 85%
 Out-of-state (17) 15%
 In-state Local (17) 62%

U.S. Microbreweries
Avg. Percent Sales that are . . .
 Self-distributed (76) 46%
 Distributor (76) 54%
Avg. No. of Distributors (69) 8.0
Avg. Percent Sales that are . . .
 In-state (89) 88%
 Out-of-state (89) 12%
 In-state Local (89) 70%

Contract Brewing Companies
Avg. Percent Sales that are . . .
 Self-distributed (27) 16%
 Distributor (27) 84%
Avg. No. of Distributors (26) 29.1
Avg. Percent Sales that are . . .
 In-state (26) 37%
 Out-of-state (26) 63%

Table 9
Sales Distribution: by type of account

U.S. Brewpubs
Avg. % Beer Sold...
- on Premises (95) 93%
- at Liquor/Grocery Stores (91) 1%
- at Bars/Restaurants (not self) (94) 5%

Canadian Brewpubs
Avg. % Beer Sold...
- on Premises (24) 98%
- at Liquor/Grocery Stores (23) 0%
- at Bars/Restaurants (not self) (24) 2%

U.S. Microbreweries
Avg. % Beer Sold...
- on Premises (74) 13%
- at Liquor/Grocery Stores (66) 30%
- at Bars/Restaurants (not self) (73) 57%

Canadian Microbreweries
Avg. % Beer Sold...
- on Premises (18) 7%
- at Liquor/Grocery Stores (17) 47
- at Bars/Restaurants (not self) (18) 44%

Contract Brewing Companies
Avg. % Beer Sold...
- at Liquor/Grocery Stores (25) 59%
- at Bars/Restaurants (not self) (25) 41%

Microbreweries

Generally speaking, a microbrewery needs four attributes to be successful: good financing, a quality product, a consistent product, and appropriate marketing.

In looking at the industry-wide figures of bottled beer sales versus draft, one sees that microbreweries generally sell about 50 percent of their beer in draft form. (See Table 7.) This is in contrast to the entire brewing industry. In the U.S. about 11 percent of total domestic beer sales is draft. For the Canadian industry the figure is 9 percent.

U.S. microbreweries sell an average of 88 percent of their beer in-state and on average utilize eight distributors. (See Table 8.) This can be compared with contract brewing companies, which sell an average of 37 percent of their product in-state and average twenty-nine distributors.

Table 9 illustrates the types of accounts where these beers are sold.

When you start a microbrewery, you had best keep the beer local initially. Keep your selling and shipping costs low by keeping sales close to the brewery location. Beer, by nature, is a perishable product, and a brewery encounters a whole new set of problems when it ships beer far from home. The benefits of selling beer locally are twofold: your profit margin is greater than when you ship, and your consumers are assured fresh product.

Microbreweries' competition, besides being other microbreweries and contract brewing companies, is primarily imported beer brands. The imports have enjoyed strong, consistent growth since the early 1970s, but in 1989, the import category experienced decreased sales for the first time. In 1990, the category grew but only by 0.05 percent.

The recent raise in the U.S. federal excise tax, which has affected mainly large brewers and importers, has significantly bolstered the U.S. microbrewing industry. The U.S. small brewers' exemption to the tax hike has made American microbrews much more price-competitive with imported brands than they used to be. In Canada, however, the current tax structure works against small brewers, as there is no such exemption. Canadian microbrewers face an uphill battle price-wise.

Brewpubs

First and foremost, brewpub equates with restaurant. This is essential to understand. If you are opening a brewpub, you are getting into the restaurant business.

When examining the sales in brewpubs, it is interesting to note that while the ratio of bar-to-food sales is fifty-fifty in U.S. brewpubs and sixty-forty at Canadian brewpubs, U.S. brewpubs sell on average 60 percent more beer than their Canadian counterparts. This may indicate that because U.S. brewpubs have higher food sales, their customers are staying longer—and drinking more beer. (See Table 10.)

At year end 1987, there were twenty-nine brewpubs in the U.S., half of them in California. Today, there are more than 150. States besides California where pubbreweries now proliferate include Colorado, Florida, North Carolina, and Oregon.

In 1988, thirteen brewpubs sold 1,000 barrels or more. In 1989, sixteen sold that amount or more. In 1990, thirty-four U.S. brewpubs sold 1,000 barrels or more.

The number of Canadian brewpubs has risen from seventeen to forty-three during the last three years. Ontario's industry grew the most, increasing from ten brewpubs at the end of 1987, to twenty-five by 1990. Saskatchewan is the other Canadian province enjoying growth in the segment—eight brewpubs have opened since the first was allowed in 1989.

In the U.S., brewpubs became legal in 1991 in West Virginia,

Table 10
Brewery-Restaurant Sales

U.S. Brewpubs
Avg. Check Total	(45) $12.11
Avg. Sales Ratio	(91)
Food	51%
Bar	49%
Avg. No. of Turns per Table	
Lunch	(48) 2.7
Dinner	(49) 4.2

Canadian Brewpubs
Avg. Check Total	(6) $15.75
Avg. Sales Ratio	(21)
Food	38%
Bar	62%
Avg. No. of Turns per Table	
Lunch	(8) 1.3
Dinner	(8) 2.0

U.S. Brewpubs
Avg. Amount of House Beer Sold On Site per Month   (81) 66.5bbl

Canadian Brewpubs
Avg. Amount of House Beer Sold On Site per Month   (15) 46.9hl

Avg. Amount of Guest Beers Sold On Site per Month   (18) 35bbl

Avg. Amount of Guest Beers Sold On Site per Month   (7) 25hl

Table 11
Average Price per Draft

U.S. Brewpubs
10 oz. Glass	(11) $1.56
12 oz. Glass	(33) $1.86
16 oz. Pint	(49) $2.42
64 oz. Pitcher	(29) $6.98
20 oz. Glass	(6) $3.11

Canadian Brewpubs
12 oz. Glass	(7) $2.32
16 oz. Pint	(4) $3.01
64 oz. Pitcher	(6) $9.43
20 oz. Glass	(3) $3.58

Table 12
Sales Support

U.S. Brewpubs
Avg. % Total Expenses
Allocated to Sales Support (57) 4%
Tools Used:
    Advertising 83
    Merchandise 82
    Public Relations 74
    Coasters 64
    Table Tents 50
    Posters 23
    Sales Force 18
    Packaging 16
    Incentives to Distributor 2

Canadian Brewpubs
Avg. % Total Expenses
Allocated to Sales Support (10) 6%
Tools Used:
    Public Relations 19
    Merchandise 17
    Advertising 16
    Table Tents 16
    Coasters 13
    Posters 7
    Sales Force 4

U.S. Microbreweries
Avg. % Total Expenses
Allocated to Sales Support (44) 7%
Tools Used:
    Merchandise 71
    Table Tents 69
    Posters 65
    Pub 1
Publicic Relations 58
    Sales Force 52
    Coasters 50
    Advertising 46
    Packaging 43
    Incentives to Distributor 31

Canadian Microbreweries
Avg. % Total Expenses
Allocated to Sales Support (14) 6%
Tools Used:
    Merchandise 18
    Table Tents 18
    Coasters 18
    Public Relations 17
    Posters 16
    Sales Force 15
    Advertising 14
    Packaging 13
    Incentives to Distributor 7

(CONTINUED ON PAGE 134)

Table 12
Sales Support (Continued)

Contract Brewing Companies
Avg. % Total Expenses
Allocated to Sales Support   (24) 34%
  Tools Used:
    Merchandise   26
    Table Tents   26
    Posters   23
    Public Relations   22
    Sales Force   19
    Incentives to Distributor   19
    Coasters   18
    Advertising   15
    Packaging   5

Industry-Wide Totals
  Tools Used:
    Merchandise   214
    Public Relations   190
    Table Tents   179
    Advertising   174
    Coasters   163
    Posters   134
    Sales Force   108
    Packaging   77

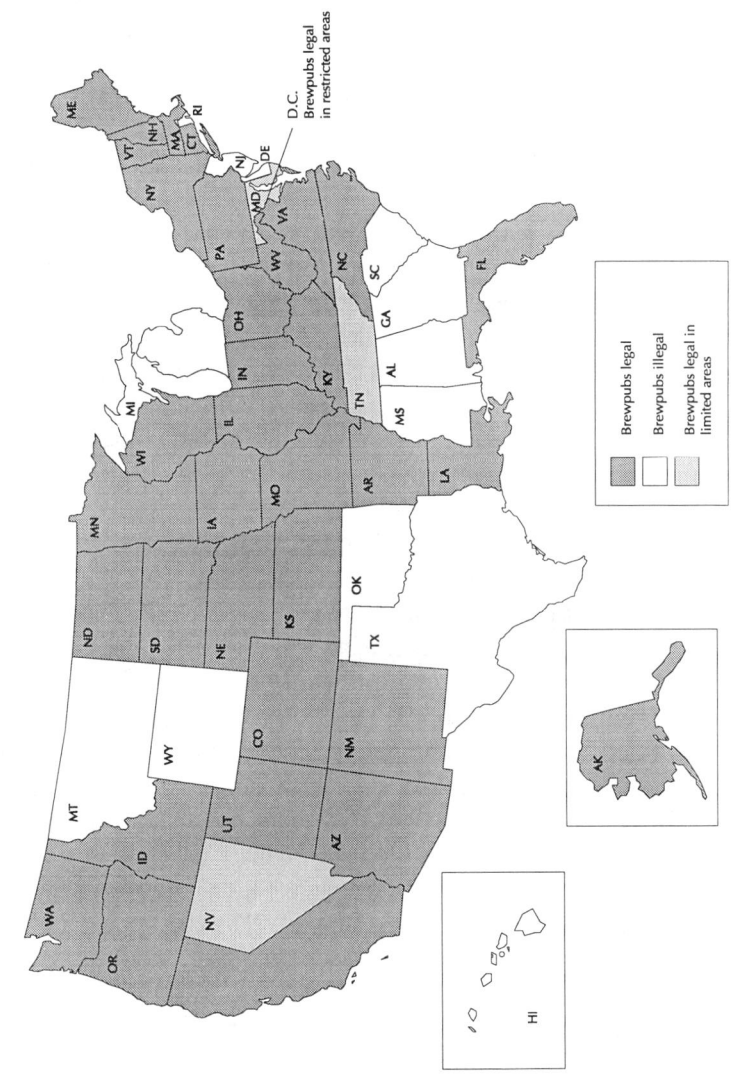

Where are Brewpubs Legal?

Arkansas, North Dakota, Nevada, Tennessee (for Memphis and Nashville only) and Washington, D.C. Brewpub legalization efforts fell short in Texas and Montana in 1991. In Canada, brewpubs are legal in every province except Yukon and Northwest Territories. (See map.)

Table 11 shows the average prices charged for brewpub beers.

Contract Brewing Companies

Contract brewing companies sometimes utilize microbreweries for the production of their beers, but most often they contract with regional or large breweries. One advantage some contract brewing companies have over microbreweries is that they are able to take advantage of the sophisticated quality control and packaging facilities and economies of scale at the larger breweries that microbreweries simply cannot afford.

Many microbreweries end up with little capital left for sales support after they finish building their brewery and working the bugs out of it. Contract brewing companies start off with a smaller investment initially and often are able to devote a greater amount of time and money to advertising and marketing their beers than most microbreweries can afford.

It is interesting to compare the average percentages of expenses allocated towards sales support and the types of sales tools used by microbreweries, brewpubs and contract brewing companies. (See Table 12.) Notice that while microbreweries and brewpubs on average apply less than 10 percent of their expenditures to sales support, contract brewing companies allocate an average of 34 percent of their funds to sales support. The most popular form of sales support for the microbrewing industry as a whole is merchandise.

While in many areas microbrewed products have opened up markets for contract-brewed beers, the opposite is true in many other areas. Contract brewing companies are successful in states without microbreweries, such as New Hampshire, Rhode Island, Delaware, Florida, Georgia, Mississippi and North Dakota. However, many contract brewed brands have proven successful at competing in markets alongside microbrewed brands.

One area in which contract brewing companies are leading the pack is exporting. According to the Institute for Brewing Studies' microbrewery database, just one microbrewed brand is being exported outside of North America, while contract brewed brands are exported to four European nations plus Japan.

Conclusion

In closing, I feel it is important to remind you that microbrewers and pubbrewers are not immune to neoprohibitionist activities. Brewers need to be proactive. Microbreweries enjoy an advantage that the largest breweries sometimes do not: they are community based. They must tune in to what is happening in their local city, county and state legislatures, lest restrictions limit people's freedom to enjoy their favorite malt beverages be placed on breweries. In addition, small brewers need to present themselves as responsible members of their local communities and help encourage consumers to exercise responsibility when drinking beer.

Despite adversities, microbreweries, brewpubs and contract brewing companies on the whole are doing extremely well. The industry will continue its dramatic growth for the next several years, at least. The progress of the craft brewing industry will continue to build on itself. Microbreweries making good beer promote other microbreweries and the industry as a whole.

As these young breweries work to educate consumers about beer—the ingredients, myriad of styles, brewing methods, history, and culture—their business will continue to grow. There is still a lot of opportunity—and many regions in this great continent that suffer from a lack of full-flavored, domestic craft-brewed beers.

Brewpubs will continue to blossom throughout the U.S. and Canada. Offering "the freshest beer in town" can be a significant advantage over other local bars and restaurants, especially when the beer is good and the local population can appreciate craft-brewed products. Brewpubs enjoy a much better survival rate than the restaurant industry does across the board.

Some 200 brewpubs have opened in North America in less than nine years. On the conservative side, it is probably a safe bet that 300 to 400 more will open during the next ten years.

David Edgar is assistant director of the Institute for Brewing Studies in Boulder, Colorado, and writes "Brew News" for **The New Brewer**. *His work has also been published in* Brewing Industry News, The Celebrator Beer News, Brewers Bulletin, All About Beer, World Beer Review *and Germany's* Brauwelt.

Chapter 11.

PACKAGING FOR THE ENVIRONMENT

*Beth Michelman Gross,
Ogilvy Adams & Rinehart*

It is a pleasure to be here representing the Glass Packaging Institute (GPI). GPI is a Washington D.C.-based trade association representing North American companies that produce glass bottles for food and beverage. GPI member companies produce more than 90 percent of the glass containers sold here in the United States. What's more of a pleasure is to be speaking to members of an industry that packages almost exclusively in glass. I call that a friendly audience. I will briefly review the benefits of the glass package and review some of the environmental and legislative issues involving glass.

Glass is a package of choice for beer and many other products for some very obvious reasons. First, glass promotes a premium image, something that is important for your business. Second, glass can be molded to meet your needs, i.e., long necks, stubbies, ten-ounce, twelve-ounce and even twenty-ounce. Third, glass is inert so there is never a problem with seepage. According to research, there are very few to no off-flavor experiences with glass, another factor that is very important to you. Also, glass is tamper-evident, so much less tampering takes place. And last, glass is 100 percent

recyclable, an extremely important consideration in today's marketplace. It is the environmental package of choice.

What do we mean by 100 percent recyclable? That means that one glass bottle can be turned into another glass bottle over and over again. No glass container ever has to go to the landfill. The term of art for this is "closed-loop" Plastic, on the other hand, is also turned into other products, but those are eventually thrown into the landfill.

According to the U.S. Department of Commerce, the federal government agrees that closed loop is the only effective recycling option. But the more pertinent question for you is, why should a brewery care about recycling?

There are several reasons, the first of which is because a solid waste crisis is occurring in this country. Landfills are filling up, and towns and municipalities nationwide are viewing recycling as a way of helping them reduce solid waste.

Second, consumers care about recycling. According to a Gallup poll, 80 percent of consumers say they will purchase a product in a recyclable container if given the choice.

Third, in the long run, glass will save you money. From a manufacturing standpoint, using *cullet*, the term for glass collected from recycling, saves wear and tear on processing furnaces, which results in savings on maintenance. This is because cullet can be melted down and reformed at lower temperatures than those required for combining virgin materials. Melting at a lower temperature saves energy and has environmental benefits as well.

For cullet to be useful, however, it must meet certain specifications. Color sorting is essential to ensure that newly manufactured containers match the color standards required by the glass container customer. For example, to make a clear bottle, we must use clear cullet.

The second concern of glass container manufacturers is contaminants such as metal caps and lids, ceramics, stones, and crystal. These contaminants are harmful because they do not melt at the same temperature used to melt the glass. Contaminants remain intact and damage the glass-melting furnace and appear as chips or bubbles in the new containers being made. Paper and plasti-shield labels are not a problem, however, and they do not need to be removed before recycling.

Given the demand for color-sorted, non-contaminated cullet, the next question is, what is the best way to collect glass for recycling? The glass container industry believes that comprehensive curbside collection is the best method. However, we also support voluntary recycling programs such as drop-off centers.

In a curbside program, citizens place bins of glass, paper, aluminum, and sometimes plastic at the curb or their regular trash pick up site.

Recycling trucks come into the neighborhood and further sort the materials. This has the added benefit of allowing operators to spot unacceptable materials easily and alert residents when they are sorting materials incorrectly.

The glass industry, however, understands that source separation may not be possible in all communities. Where source separation is not possible, the industry supports material recovery facilities (MRF). These facilities are where comingled materials are sorted and prepared for sale.

With community and industry support, recycling programs continue to grow. Curbside programs have enjoyed the most expansion with more than 2,700 programs currently operating nationwide. A recent Gallup Poll confirms consumer support for curbside recycling over other options. According to the poll, 51 percent of consumers ranked curbside as their first choice in how to fight the solid waste crisis. Meanwhile, the number of Americans willing to participate in a deposit program fell by 26 percent.

This brings us to the legislative arena and that eternal issue of forced deposits. Yes, there is national forced deposit legislation in Congress in 1991. The House bill calls for a ten-cent deposit on soft drinks, beer, wine coolers, mineral water and soda water, and mixers. The legislation is not doing well. Today there are only sixty-one cosponsors, and things seem to have lost some steam. Twenty-four states introduced deposit legislation this year.

Glass Recycles

The good news is that we have something to work for: the Comprehensive Recycling Act of 1991, which is a good bill. It calls for each state to develop its own recycling guidelines with a goal of recycling at 25 percent. Most states now have recycling laws that generally call for a percentage of waste to be recycled within a specific time frame.

Another legislative issue facing the glass container industry is recycled content. Oregon passed a law that requires each bottle sold in the state to contain 35 percent recycled glass by January 1, 1995, and 50 percent by January 1, 2000. California has passed recycled content legislation. The law requires 15 percent minimum content of bottles manufactured in the state by January 1, 1992, increasing to 65 percent in 2005. There are also proposed bills in Illinois and Kansas.

North Carolina and New Hampshire both proposed bans on green and brown bottles in their states, although neither bill passed. But as recycling picks up steam, and there is more and more cullet to be purchased, we will see more of this type of legislation.

On the positive side, there are some marketing opportunities that brewers can take advantage of that will also help to promote glass in the marketplace. We encourage you to use the "Recycling G" logo, which was developed for use on package labels. Because of consumer awareness, this logo is being used for more national brands than we ever expected. Some examples of products using the logo are Maxwell House coffee; the complete line of Pepsi Cola products; the complete line of Canada Dry products; four major national brands of applesauce; Kraft barbecue sauce; and Heinz ketchup and babyfood. We would be delighted to have brewers join us in the effort to promote recycling glass. If you are interested in using the logo on your labels, please call the Glass Packaging Institute in Washington, D.C. There are no restrictions on size, color or placement of the logo.

Each year, we hold a competition to honor excellence, innovation and environmental awareness in glass package design. The event is the Clear Choice Awards, and the winner of each category receives a star designed by Steuben glass. Last year's winner in the environmental awareness category was Hard Rock Cafe Beer, and the award was accepted by the general manager of the Chicago Hard Rock Cafe. We encourage all of you to enter.

Beer is a truly important segment of the glass container industry. We look forward to working with the microbrewery industry to meet your needs.

Beth Michelman Gross is senior associate at Ogilvy Adams and Rinehart Public Affairs in Washington, D.C., where she manages the account of the Glass Packaging Institute. She directs the marketing and press efforts for GPI's environmental awareness, industry outreach and direct marketing.

Chapter 12.

MULTI-UNIT OPERATIONS

*Dean Biersch,
Gordon Biersch Brewing Co.*

As my partners and I currently operate only two brewery restaurants in the San Francisco Bay Area, I am not sure how qualified I am to present my comments regarding multi-unit operations, but I am pleased to comment on the challenges we have faced in growing our small company these past few years.

I would guess that many among you have achieved some degree of success with your first project and naturally have begun to look forward to new ventures. Perhaps you, like me, have searched the industry media for information on restaurant expansion formulas and found little useful information on the subject. Though there is some information to be found here and there, for the most part each of us has to learn in our own way. In my experience, I have found it more useful to hear or read how someone has developed his or her business, and take what I can to apply to my own business. In that spirit, what follows is simply the approach we at Gordon Biersch have taken to grow our company.

Gordon Biersch Brewing Company

Let me begin with a little background on our company. My

partner, Dan Gordon, and I founded Gordon Biersch Brewing Company in 1987. My background was in corporate food-service operations, and Dan was a recent graduate of the five-year Brewing Engineering program at Weihenstephan in Freising, Germany. Our first brewery restaurant was opened in July 1988, in downtown Palo Alto, a suburb south of San Francisco and adjacent to Stanford University. We opened our second store in downtown San Jose, thirty-two miles to the south, in April 1990. A third Gordon Biersch project is currently under construction on the Embarcadero in San Francisco, thirty-five miles to the north, and is scheduled to open in February 1992. Gordon Biersch is a full-service, restaurant-and-brewery concept featuring a wide variety of cuisines and German style beers including Export, Märzen and Dunkles.

Food and beverage sales for the Palo Alto store started at $2.2 million per year and have increased to $2.7 million for the past two years. First year sales for San Jose were $3.3 million. Gordon Biersch currently produces and sells about 1,600 barrels per year in Palo Alto and 2,400 barrels per year in San Jose. All beer sales are by the glass. Both breweries produce at maximum capacity, so consequently we handle no draft or bottle accounts.

From One Unit to Two: The Basics

With that in mind, let's advance to what I perceive are the basic and fundamental prerequisites to moving beyond your single unit to a multi-unit operation. Of primary importance is the establishment of a solid, standard accounting system that includes:
- Daily bookkeeping and cash handling procedures
- Daily sales breakdowns and related productivity reports
- Monthly profit and loss and balance sheet reports
- Yearly audits of the corporation or partnership.

Filling the daily bookkeeping position should have been a given for us, but we almost blew it in the beginning. We spent so much energy and money on getting the dream built that we gave little consideration to how we would handle the incoming cash. We were fortunate to find someone at the last moment, and very shortly thereafter we recognized what a key position this person plays in our daily operations. This is the person you trust with your cash, your reputation with various vendors, your commercial banker, and others, so do the background checks and watch the books closely.

You all should be aware of the importance of monitoring your daily sales breakdowns. This is information you now have that you could only speculate about when you wrote your original business plan. Remember scratching your head and trying to figure how many liters of beer you would sell on a rainy Monday in February? Now you know. Knowing your month-to-month fluctuations, percentages of food to beverage sales, server productivity, which food specials and beer styles sell better than others: these are critically useful data you can use in planning your next unit.

Your profit-and-loss statement is your scorecard. Gordon Biersch has a policy of presenting our P-and-L to our managers (not just the general manager) within ten days of the end of each month. We compare percentages to industry standards and those set by our company. After your first year of business, you can compare the figures with those of the previous year. Have your managers sign a non-disclosure agreement and show them the numbers. Through this knowledge, managers gain a real-time perspective of restaurant operations and learn to respect the comprehensive effort it takes to turn a profit in this business. Your primary intent should be to develop the same concern for costs in your management staff that you yourself have. Goals can be established and priorities set by reviewing this statement with your management staff.

As we have plans to someday sell our company, we have established a policy of having our books formally audited at the conclusion of each fiscal year. Audits are expensive, and we paid around

$15,000 for our last one, but there is a great deal to be gained from them. A good audit lets you (and your banker) know exactly where you stand; it potentially shows nefarious accounting practices; and it provides—as part of the service—professional advice on improving your current accounting systems. Then, when you go to your banker to extend your existing line of credit for your new store, you will at least get the meeting if you forward your most recent audit. Also, a continuous series of audits, verses one or two, makes your numbers more credible to a potential buyer should you decide to sell. So, get your fiscal house in order, then move on to creating your next unit.

Using Your Existing Facility

I have already alluded to this point; be sure to fully exploit your existing location when establishing a new one. None of us has time to relearn our mistakes made in the past and adding another operation will present enough new problems as it is.

Like most restaurant companies, we have found that providing an interesting, structured and enjoyable place of employment is key to our ability to expand. We all want to attract and cultivate the finest management and employees we can find. Under the best circumstances, this is never an easy proposition. But the whole process can be handled much more effectively when you have an existing base of operations.

Potential new hires can now come in and see firsthand what you are all about. We encourage them to talk to our employees about our employees' opinion of our employment practices. If we are considering hiring a new *sous* chef, we pay him to come in and work the line for a few shifts. In this way, we get the opportunity to observe his skills, and he gets to experience our working conditions. These are things we could never do before we opened the first restaurant.

The physical layout of your existing operation should also be analyzed and the appropriate questions asked. Should your next store have more bar seating? Is there a better way to light your new space? What have you learned about seating and table sizes? What can you learn from your bar manager and executive chef? What do the servers have to say about your point-of-sale system? Do your hosts like the phone system? These are the kinds of things you should explore with your staff before you begin the design stage of your new unit. You will never get the same results from a consultant that you can from your own staff.

Sell Growth

When you add a unit, you are potentially doubling your growth, and so your next step is to go out and sell that growth. If you have already established your own company, you are fully aware of the professional assistance you required to open the doors. Architects, lawyers, accountants, brewery manufacturers, designers, graphic designers, general contractors, mechanical engineers and many more will be involved in your new project. Many of these will be able to assist (assuming you want to use them again!) in ways they couldn't the first time around. Once you have gained experience with them—and they with your operation, you both should now begin the work of saving dollars. For example, my partner and I like to use a design-engineering approach to construction where we present to our subcontractors a "not-to-exceed" budget number. Once we reach agreement on the cost, we receive a guaranteed maximum from the sub and we get to sleep at night.

When selecting an architectural firm for our new San Francisco project, we paid a nominal amount to four different firms to have them present design ideas for the space and compete for the job. This gave us the opportunity to get more minds involved in space planning, and though we selected only one, lots of useful ideas were generated in the process.

You should also consider that some of the professional trades will be interested in trading services rendered on the project for equity in your company. We have been successful in getting brewery manufacturers and mechanical engineers to provide equipment and services in this way. I have heard that large grocery vendors can often be approached as well. After all, they have firsthand experience with the volume of your purchases and your payment record.

Finally, if your company has been established with the intention of growing into a multi-unit operation, you will find many professionals willing to cut normal costs in order to have an opportunity to work with you in the future.

Establish Quality Vendor Relationships — And Renegotiate

As in any business wishing to grow, it is critical to establish quality vendor relationships from the beginning. Assuming you have done so, you should now take the opportunity to renegotiate your agreements.

At Gordon Biersch we like to use specialty vendors for such products as bread, coffee and linen. The primary reason is that we enjoy working with other small businesses like ours, rather than the big guys. You may pay a bit more in the beginning, but you will usually find a higher degree of personal service and quicker response times, and it is simply more fun to spend your money with a company that benefits more directly from your own growth. When it comes time to expand your volume, remember to go to these people and renegotiate your current contracts.

Don't overlook the big guys however; as our business has grown, we have been able to leverage our growth with various vendors such as contract cleaners, sanitation product suppliers and others.

Your Next Location

In discussing your moving on to a second location, I will assume that you know your market well and are willing to stake your existing reputation on it. For our second unit, we wanted a building that would offer the physical layout we required and be located in an area that would be receptive to our services. Our new location needed to be supported from our existing base of operations, and yet not cannibalize our existing guest base.

From our reservation list in Palo Alto, we soon discovered that lots of guests were coming from the telephone area code to the south. We also drew a lot of corporate business from that area. We felt that with that consumer awareness as a running start, and our perception of the new location as being in a demographically separate market, we could draw both those people familiar with Gordon Biersch and also build a new base of clientele.

Also, we are fortunate to live and work in a very mobile area so that many of our patrons may live in close proximity to one location and work in the other, or visa versa, and we are able to get them to visit both.

It is useful to make up a worksheet for the various commercial real estate brokers you will use. In addition to physical space requirements and the commercial style of the building you desire, be sure to let them know your anticipated mechanical loads, parking requirements, and the percentages of production-to-retail space you are anticipating.

Both of our new locations are within half-an-hour drive of our first store and corporate offices. In my opinion, this is a very manageable distance. Our success in moving beyond the three units will be a product of our ability to develop our management team.

Management Structure

Clearly, our greatest challenge to new growth is the development, training and retention of quality management. With our intention of adding a second and third unit within our first few years of operations, we decided to carry from the outset a little extra management. Developing a small company such as ours can create stress at the management level. With an additional manager of staff, we can soften the schedule at bit, provide a five-day work week, honor requests for vacations and leaves of absence, and so on.

As my partner and I have gotten more and more involved in new project development, we needed the assurance that day-to-day operations would continue to receive direct management input. When we added the second unit, we promoted our first general manager to the position of director of restaurant operations. Our general managers report directly to this person. One of the operation director's key duties is to ensure that job descriptions and training manuals exist for all positions in the restaurant. This director also is responsible for developing and training the existing management staff.

On the kitchen side of operations, we have an executive chef, who oversees the head chefs at each unit. We want to have one person responsible for the organization and operation of each kitchen unit. Recipes need to be standardized and systems established for inventory control and rotation; for example, purchasing is coordinated on a number of items. In the first year of operating the second store, we found that we could not afford to carry an executive chef and two head chefs, so our executive chef held the position of head chef in one store, in addition to his other duties.

With our third unit, we will soon add management personnel in the positions of development director and chief financial officer. The development director's responsibilities will include specifications development, site selection, lease negotiations, construction negotiations, and project management for all new facilities. He or she will report to the owners and will work closely with the operations director to ensure that valuable lessons learned from the operating facilities are incorporated into future facilities.

In addition to creating a solid management structure for your operations, you should consider the importance of establishing a management style for your company. This has to do with establishing the unique way in which you conduct your business. Without going into the details of our approach, I can say that your management team must be clear about your (the owner's) goals and expectations for the business. This must include the standards and procedures you set for attaining those goals.

Remember that in the area of management relations, it is your responsibility to listen to the desires of your staff and when possible create opportunities for their growth within the organization. Be aware of the time period when your managers come up for salary reviews. Spend time getting to know them and which projects they find personally fulfilling. In short, respect the efforts they bring to your cause and reward them when they have earned it.

Communication

In addition to having a solid management model in place to ensure that systems are followed and quality assured, you must quickly learn to appreciate the importance of establishing strong lines of communication.

There is no way you will be able to devote twelve-plus hours of undivided attention to your new stores the way you did with your first unit. We have found that regular two-to-three hour, weekly meetings at each unit are necessary to ensure that we are progressing and solving problems. Attendance is mandatory. The meeting are hosted by the general manager and are attended by the:

- Owners
- Director of operations
- Executive chef

- General manager
- Head chef
- Floor management
- Bar management
- Bookkeeping

Our format for these meetings includes at least the following:
- Quality control issues
- Evaluation of budget and projections
- Maintenance issues
- Upcoming functions
- Scheduling issues and schedule projections
- Employee status reports
- General and unusual situations
- Open forum
- Setting goals and objectives

Beyond the discussion of fundamental business issues, the weekly meeting is a good forum for you to encourage and motivate your management staff. Our managers are always interested in hearing the latest news about new projects, money-raising efforts and so on. Dan and I make it our responsibility to give them an update on the "big picture" at least once a week. I have found it very useful to explain what I am actually doing when I am head-long into project development. Don't assume your employees understand why you are not around as much as you used to be.

When you can, you should try to make every effort to involve all your key staff members, as much as possible, in the growth of the company. We pay our management staff to go out and scout all the competitors in the area of our new location. This is a fun, little perk for them, and the information they bring back on everything from the cleanliness of the bathrooms, to the style of service, to the timing between courses is invaluable information for the company. Under the same format we require each manager to eat at least once a month at the Gordon Biersch restaurant where they do not regularly work. Their reviews are part of the quality control segment at the start of each weekly meeting. All Gordon Biersch managers are also encouraged to eat out, with a guest, once a month in a Bay Area restaurant that we feel we can learn from.

Getting back to the importance of communication, if you cannot be present on location, you need to find ways of making yourself available to your management group. Dan and I encourage all managers to call us directly if they have a problem or think we should know about something. We use car phones because we are on the road a lot. And each of us down through the general manager level has a Macintosh computer with a modem at home so that files can be transferred and memos sent. Within the restaurant, we make heavy use of fax machines and a special Watts line to keep down phone costs.

The busier you get, the more you will begin to rely on the information you get from others. You will not always be there to see firsthand what is happening. I have found that I need to be very specific with the questions I ask of my managers. Instead of asking how the lunch shift went, I ask how many servers we used, when we got the big rush, what kind of special the chef offered, how the food looked at a corporate function, and so on. If there were problems, I try to identify how they might be handled in the future and make note of them for group discussion at the next management meeting.

In an effort to increase your understanding of your operations, you should consider enlisting shopping and spotter services. A *shopper service* is a company that sends out diners to your establishment for the purpose of comprehensively evaluating your operation from the viewpoint of a guest. The diners check everything from how easily your signage is read from the street, to how they were greeted, how quickly their coffee cup was refilled, the server's description of the daily specials, and how clean the bathrooms were.

A *spotter service* does the same thing, but its focus is primarily on the bar area and cash-handling procedures. Spotters tell you if a bartender is giving away beer, taking cash without ringing the proper amount, or talking with his buddies at the end of the bar while guests are waiting to be served.

Use of these services is a prudent way to control and understand our business. All of our employees know these services are being used, and we always give them an opportunity to give their side of the story before we take action on the reports. All reports are posted, with names blackened out, for the entire staff to read.

Translating Your Concept to a New Location

Let's discuss whether you should, when adding a second unit, try to copy your existing location or change the concept in some way. Operationally, as I have noted, you want to make as many improvements to the new facility as possible. But the question is, should you stick with what you know or alter your concept?

This is a question only the operator can answer. We felt comfortable making only a few subtle changes. Regarding our menu, we wanted to offer the standard, proven items that we had established in our first store, but we also wanted to give our new chef the flexibility to design his own menu. Our guests would expect to have the same style of beers in both stores, so we wouldn't consider changing that. We wanted to create an atmosphere that was familiar to guests who knew our first store, but we also wanted to add variety and new seating situations. In short, we wanted to establish a comfort level that was familiar but with a few added twists. So in San Jose, we built an outdoor courtyard and a separate corporate entertaining room. We added a weekly jazz series and live music a couple of nights a week. Our menu there is clearly more directed to Asian influences. We hope this has given potential guests an option when considering dining in either of our establishments.

Before You Open Number Two: Public Relations

As you know, our industry is an interesting and topical subject for the various local, regional and national media. This is not typical of your standard restaurant operation, and you are missing a great opportunity if you do not exploit this important difference. Make a special effort to generate interest from various media before you open your new store. Our ability to fill our restaurant from the beginning in a formerly marginal downtown location was almost entirely a result of the publicity we were able to generate and the goodwill we were able to establish with our existing location.

The Problems of Growth

I have attempted to outline a good, working formula for those of you wishing to expand your brewpub operations, but I also want to go over some of the pitfalls you can expect to encounter in that process.

Probably the most difficult thing to accept is the loss of intimacy you had with your first store. Starting a business like this is not unlike having your first child; all the time you spent with its inception—though very tough and trying—was done willingly and naturally. But just wait until you walk into one of your restaurants and are greeted by an employee you have never met! I have had an employee ask me if I wanted smoking or nonsmoking, and another employee asked if I had come to train for the new busser position.

I don't think you can go back to the way it was in the beginning. What I try to do now is spend as much time as possible on the restaurant floor with my employees. I try to make myself available.

I show them I still know how to seat a guest or bus a table. Beyond that, I try to provide leadership.

Consider that your employees also need to be kept informed of the development process the company is going through. Speak to them directly at staff meetings and company parties. Ask for their direct input on problems you are attempting to solve. Your kitchen and floor staff often have the best solutions.

Another change from your previous work routine will be the increased proportion of time you spend in meetings. Sometimes I think all I do now is sit in on meetings. I have yet to figure a way around these things. Naturally, you will be able to grow at a faster pace if you can effectively direct your meetings. Prepare an agenda and keep the group on track.

Finally, expect that there will be unforeseen problems on your horizon. When we opened San Jose, we were hit with 300 percent more volume than we expected. The first weekend, we ran out of food and had to close. The kitchen was woefully undersized. The bathrooms were being totally abused. The brewery would never be able to keep up. So, on top of all the little surprises an opening brings, in the first week we had to order four new fermentation tanks, start new architectural drawings for an additional two restrooms, and convert two existing restrooms to a kitchen prep area. It was six months before we were able to catch up. In the process, we were very concerned that our restaurant in Palo Alto would suffer from lack of attention. Many of our employees there felt that we had abandoned them. So for all your planning and organization, things never fall out the way you anticipated. Have an alternate plan—and that usually means restructuring your management to ensure that you don't lose control of what you already have.

The Benefits of Growth

Let me conclude by discussing a few benefits of growth. For

me, one of the great satisfactions of growth is pulling out the old business plans and seeing how close to the mark we were on our early assumptions and projections. It is very gratifying to know that your ideas are worthy and can be translated into a model that works.

Having multi-unit operations allows you much more flexibility when it comes to attracting the best employees, professionals and vendors. The second time around, you have much more leverage and a reputation as an operator. You are able to give your employees more flexibility by allowing them to work in various locations, and you can realistically offer growth to those employees who want to move up in the company. You have heightened your understanding of your business patterns so maybe you can rest a little easier at night. With this pattern of growth, you can continue to establish a foundation for the future.

Finally, let me sum up by saying that in order to succeed in this business, you need to embrace problem-solving every day. When problems pop up, you need to recognize them, determine the best solution, and get busy with remedying them. For those who can get into that never-ending practice, relax and enjoy because with each new unit you get to make a whole new bunch of mistakes!

Dean Biersch supervises the restaurant operations for Gordon Biersch Brewing Company, which was established in 1987. His background includes food service management positions with the Beverly Hilton Hotel in Beverly Hills and Hornblower Dining Yachts in San Francisco.

Chapter 13.

THE MARKETING OF DRAFT VS. BOTTLED BEER

*Peter McAuslan,
Brasserie McAuslan*

There are three major avenues for the sale of beer: packaged beer for on-premise consumption; draft beer for on-premise consumption; and packaged beer for off-premise consumption. Other important avenues for sales are direct brewery sales (beer sold in brewery retail stores) and contract brewing. This discussion will focus primarily on the first three options with comments on the others.

Factors Impacting Market Strategies

Within any state or province, the marketing behavior of brewers is shaped by several significant factors such as alcohol legislation, taxation, competition, and the socio-demographic characteristics of the population in a specific market area.

Legislation. Government regulation has major impact on brewers' marketing strategies. In some jurisdictions, a brewer is required to charge a customer for point-of-sale (POS) materials such as coasters and table tents. In other jurisdictions, brewers cannot only give away such items without charge, they can also provide draft systems and significant volumes of free beer. Yet, they are

forbidden to give free beer samples to the public. Thus, legislation shapes marketing and the competitive environment in ways the brewer must take into consideration when he or she is planning market strategies.

Taxation. In Canada, tax can represent more than half the retail cost of beer, whereas in the United States, it can be as low as 19 percent. In Canada, alcohol tax is determined on production volumes; it is hidden in the cost of the product to the retailer and subsequently marked up. As a result, the price difference in Canada between premium and regular beer is much smaller than in the U.S. As a result, taxation defines price and therefore has a strong impact on marketing.

Competition. A brewer's marketing behavior varies depending on the competition. If a brewery is the only producer in a state or a province, it markets differently than if it is in direct competition with other microbreweries, large brewers, or a significant volume of imports.

Socio-Demographic Characteristics. A brewer must know who the potential customers are in a particular market in order to address them. A new company should expend money and effort to define the needs and characteristics of the target market.

Once the brewer is aware of the major factors shaping the marketing environment, he or she can explore specific plans for the three major sales avenues.

The Marketing of Draft vs. Bottled Beer

Those planning a microbrewery must decide whether to produce beer on draft only, or to produce both draft and bottled beer. In making the decision, there are many questions to be answered. A few are discussed briefly below.

What are the characteristics of the market? Is it urban or rural? Is draft beer strong in the market or is the market dominated by bottled beer? Is the market already occupied by other microbreweries who produce draft beer that is strong in the best locations? The answers to these questions can help the potential brewer make a sound judgment on the draft vs. bottle issue.

What is the planned brewery capacity? A brewery with a low capital cost, a single product and a bottling operation must sell a minimum of 4,250 barrels (5,000 hectolitres), or about 60,000 cases, to reach the break-even point. Yet, it is possible for a draft-only brewery to reach break-even at significantly lower sales volumes.

The brewer who wants to bottle must have a brewhouse capable of producing 4,250 barrels (5,000 hl), but pragmatically, he or she should start with a capacity of 10,000 barrels (11,000 hl) or face constant renovation and refinancing.

What are the brewery's long term goals? Draft-only operations are limited to markets comparatively close to the brewery. Competition for taps in bars is tough and expensive. The growth of a draft-only brewery is limited by these factors. The brewer who wants to have long-term growth must consider bottling from the outset, even if the bottling operation is to be added later. In such instances, the brewer must have at least three times the space required for the draft-only operation.

What is the budget? A bottling operation adds a minimum of $200,000 in capital expense and start-up capital needs and also significantly increases the operating costs of staffing, marketing, sales, and distribution. Conversely, the payment for bottled products can be slow and a strain on the company's cash flow. The brewer must foresee this factor to avoid financial catastrophe.

Marketing Strategies

Once the decision is made on draft vs. bottle, specific marketing strategies can be developed. The effective marketing of microbrewery products is almost as important as the quality and style of the beer itself. The task is complex and involves all marketing disciplines: sales, promotion, advertising, and public relations. Specific strategies can and should be defined for marketing on-premise vs. off-premise sales, but to be effective, the marketing plan must be comprehensive and result in the sale of beer in one environment supporting the sale in the other environments. Brand awareness by consumers sells beer, and this is created by many small repeated contacts between the buyer and the brewery.

For this presentation thirty-seven breweries across Canada and the U.S. were surveyed on their marketing practices. Seventeen breweries (six Canadian and eleven American) responded. Their annual production ranged from 900 barrels to 15,500 barrels, with fourteen of them producing more than 4,000 barrels. All respondents with the exception of one sells both bottled and draft beer.

Marketing Draft Beer

A majority of small brewers consider sales of draft beer to have greater profit margins than bottled beer and also provide an important marketing tool for selling bottled beer. Brewers go to significant lengths to add draft accounts and even more to keep them. In conversation, brewers cite the necessity of providing fresh beer and excellent service and developing close relationships with the client.

Accounts are added by providing lower cost and better quality products than the competition (most frequently the imports), and also by offering product incentives including introductory product at low or, in some cases, no cost. Key POS items such as tent cards and coasters, and special events such as "beer evening" promotions, are essential in supporting the product to the consumer on an on-going basis. A strong relationship between the brewer and client can be created through providing special services such as instruction on draft system troubleshooting or beer seminars for staff.

Brewers frequently cited marketing tools for the sale of draft as:
- Excellent service
- Fresh beer
- Positive relationship with bar owner and staff
- Price promotions
- On-site product events
- Tastings
- Table tents specifying specials

On-Premise Sales of Bottled Beer

Marketing bottled beer on-premise is a challenge for the microbrewer because it is difficult to compete with the highly advertised brands of the major breweries. The key is being able to stand out among the numerous brands of bottled beer at the on-premise location. Strong marketing effort is required for these sales as sales both contribute to overall brewery volumes and support off-premise sales.

Most frequently cited marketing tools for on-premise bottle sales are:
- Volume discounts
- Relationship with bar owner/staff
- Price promotions
- Effective POS materials, particularly table tents
- On-location product promotion

Off-Premise Sales of Bottled Beer

Most beer sold by North American brewers is for off-premise consumption, and therefore the marketing program of a brewery ultimately succeeds or fails on its generation of sales in this critical area. The brand awareness created by major brewers cannot be matched on a national level by the microbrewer. However, the microbrewer can develop a brand profile in a limited market area in order to create high-volume sales. This can only occur if a program integrates an effective sales team, sales strategy, promotional program of event sponsorship, and effective use of a limited advertising budget. If this is done well, a brewer's product can be omnipresent in the targeted area, and the brewer can benefit from the cumulative marketing effect or synergy.

The brewers surveyed reported the following strategies for off-premise sales:
- Effective overall marketing program
- Excellent service and positive relationship with staff/manager
- Price discounts on volume
- Effective POS materials
- Presence of bottle beer at on-premise locations
- Tastings

Marketing Tools

I cannot overemphasize that beer sales require an effective, integrated marketing program. The following represents information provided by the seventeen responding breweries on various aspects of their marketing.

Brand Name and Logo. The most important marketing decisions involve the choice of a product name and logo. Both must appeal to the market segment being targeted. Microbreweries do not have large budgets and are mostly unable to buy television or even significant print advertising. Therefore, the beer's name must be memorable and the logo must have high visual impact to be effective. Microbrewers must choose bold packaging that works.

Sales Force. In Canada and the U.S., beer is generally distributed by wholesalers or through government and/or brewery-owned monopolies. Regardless of the sales and distribution structure, brewery salesforces seem to be based on a ratio of one person per 2,800 barrels of sales in the U.S. and one person per 2,600 hl of sales in Canada.

One-third of the breweries surveyed have their staff focus exclusively on bar and restaurant accounts, while two-thirds have their people cover all accounts.

POS Materials. All breweries use POS materials to support the sales of their products. It is no surprise that virtually all breweries use similar types of items. The seven most popular items evaluated for marketing effectiveness by Canadian and American brewers are listed below in order of effectiveness:

American	Canadian
• T-shirts	• Posters
• Table tents	• Table tents
• Coasters	• Coasters
• Posters	• Other clothing *
• Glasses	• T-shirts
• Other clothing *	• Bar Umbrellas
• Bar Umbrellas	• Glasses

* Hats are the other clothing item most frequently mentioned.

The majority of breweries use beer glasses but evaluate them as a very ineffective marketing tool. Bar umbrellas are not frequently used (probably as a result of their cost), but they are evaluated very highly by those who use them. The same is true of neon signs, which are infrequently used by micros but which are very effective according to those who do.

Media Usage. The usage of print, television and radio by microbreweries is minimal and not considered very effective.

Print advertising is the most frequently used medium and is

focused primarily in community and alternative newspapers. Approximately 70 percent of brewers advertise in these papers and evaluate the exposure as being moderately effective. Local magazines also attract some advertising dollars but are rated as being moderately ineffective.

A minority of brewers use television (community or cable) and consider this ineffective. Private radio is used more frequently and is considered effective.

Overall, the media is used sparsely and is never considered as effective as the use of other marketing activities. Brewers using media select only those types that attract a high percentage of potential consumers of microbrewery products.

Public Relations and the Media. The low use of media advertising notwithstanding, free media coverage is one of the marketing cornerstones of the small brewery industry. Free publicity gives the small brewer exposure, profile and credibility. As the coverage is editorial in nature, it is likely to be read and believed by the public. This is not always the case with paid advertising.

In the August issue of *Modern Beverage Age*, a beer importer was quoted as saying that the microbreweries get too much exposure given the size of the market. He is underestimating the level of interest the public is showing in our industry. Small brewers get heavy coverage because we represent independent free enterprisers in a David-and-Goliath struggle with the large brewers and importers. We are producers of high-quality, "natural" beers that are truly distinctive, and also, we are community based, not national or multi-national companies. These are very positive issues, and the smart brewer always attempts to promote these assets by maintaining excellent product standards and keeping a high level of contact with the media.

Event Sponsorship. All microbrewers surveyed are heavily involved in community sports, cultural and social activities. The

small brewer is important in the community and relies upon reciprocal support. Brewers evaluate each proposed activity in the following terms:
- Increased product awareness
- Generation of goodwill and consumer loyalty
- Market development
- Cost vs. benefit

Brewers do not sponsor events for altruistic reasons alone. In many instances, brewers participate because they believe they will attract to their product a number of first-time tasters. Yet, in event sponsorship, the brewer must define by written agreement exactly what promotional benefits are to accrue as a result of participating, and he or she should provide event management to see that these agreements are carried out. Following is a discussion of various events brewers tend to help sponsor.

Sports Event Sponsorship. Most frequently, microbreweries support community running, skiing, sailing, and swimming events. They tend to support more esoteric sports such as masters swimming, rugby, soccer, and polo and even "ultimate frisbee," footbag and backgammon.

All of these activities have certain things in common: They are less "mainstream," and they attract many non-traditional athletes. In short, they are somewhat eccentric. These characteristics are not unlike those of our industry and our products.

Sponsorship often involves a number of different factors including exclusive use of the brewery sponsor's product at the social events associated with the sport. For the brewer, the profile accorded its identity has value, but the real value is having beer tasted by many "first timers," thereby building a loyal clientele.

Community Events. Small brewers are heavily involved in all aspects of community life from fund raisers for food and shelters to support of medical and environmental research. Once again, the key for the brewer is higher profile, the generation of goodwill, and a whole flock of first-time tasters.

Cultural events. Small brewers support live theater, local symphony orchestras, and music festivals from chamber music to jazz to new age. Art galleries receive support, and at least one small brewer has a special price for student artist first shows. Student film-making is well supported, frequently in exchange for product visibility. Small brewers occasionally sponsor local and international film festivals as well.

Food, wine and beer shows. Most small brewers participate in trade shows where they can give samples or sell single servings of their products. Although these shows can be comparatively expensive, they are viewed as being effective because they attract a high proportion of consumers who are interested in specialty products.

Brewery tours. Virtually all of the breweries surveyed conduct brewery tours, and approximately one-third use slide or video presentations as part of the tour. Tours combined with brewery stores can create large numbers of first-time buyers. Positive tour experiences create customers, while brewery stores create profitable immediate sales.

Marketing Budgets

The average marketing budget of the seventeen breweries surveyed was 8.5 percent of sales. Marketing costs included sales staff, advertising, POS materials, and the retail value of promotional beer given to retailers or to the public at tastings or sponsorship events. Budgets for brewers who bottle beer are higher than those with draft-only producers.

Contract Brewing

About one-quarter of U.S. and Canadian microbrewers are

offering contract brewing services. Generally this is restricted to private label bottled or draft brands for hotels and restaurant chains, but some brewers are producing bottled product for off-premise sales as well. Those brewers involved with private label brewing report marginally higher margins as they do not incur the sales, distribution and marketing costs for these products.

Conclusion

The decision to sell draft and/or bottled beer impacts all aspects of a brewery from brewhouse design to marketing. The draft-only brewer has to develop a much higher concentration of high-volume accounts in a smaller geographic region than his bottling colleague. On-premise marketing strategies employed are the same as those of the brewer of draft and bottled beer but have to be more frequent and intense at the point of sale for the draft brewery to succeed.

The brewer of bottled beer must develop marketing strategies for on-premise and off-premise sales that reflect the needs of these different environments, but these strategies must be integrated in order to provide overall support for the sales effort. Only the effective integration of these strategies generate the sales volumes that leads to profitability for the brewer who has taken up the challenge of producing bottled beer.

Peter McAuslan founded McAuslan Brewing Inc., in Montreal, Quebec, in 1988, and is president and CEO of that company as well as of an associated venture capital firm. He is also president of the Quebec Association of Microbrewers and vice president of the Canadian Independent Brewers Association. He lives in Hudson, Quebec with his brewmaster wife, Ellen Bounsall.

Chapter 14.

THE BUSINESS OF BREWING

Jim Koch, Boston Beer Co.
Paul Shipman, Redhook Ale Brewery

The following dialogue occurred during a round-table discussion where Paul Shipman and Jim Koch fielded questions.

Question: *Paul, has the taste of your beer changed at all during the growth of your brewery?*

Paul Shipman: I can taste a difference, I don't know exactly how to describe it, but I think it's a combination of an extremely vigorous boil and close process control that has had a definite, positive impact on the product. We also had a change in management in the brewing operation when Al Triplett took over the brewery in 1988. I think proper management has a greater impact on the quality of beer than the equipment does. It's also a lot easier to manage the newer, higher-technology equipment than it was to work with the old equipment. However, the old equipment was a great way to start a microbrewery.

Question: *Jim, can you comment on Tom Potter's experiences with distribution? (See Chapter 8.)*

Jim Koch: There's very little Tom said that I don't find a lot of

truth in. At this point, we sell our beer through about 200 wholesalers. I would second Tom's comment that deciding whether or not to self-distribute and choosing your distributors are among the most important decisions you make.

For us, the big concern is freshness, which is a concern for everybody. You should bear in mind that product freshness is independent of the distance from the brewery to the market. We can get Samuel Adams into any market where we sell in less than twenty-four hours shipping time. Beer doesn't go bad between the brewery and the wholesaler unless you've really screwed up. It goes bad somewhere in the distribution. What this means is that you're fooling yourself if you say, "We only sell locally, in the shadow of the brewhouse. So all our beer is fresh." Beer gets stale if wholesalers and retailers have too much inventory or if they fail to rotate it. That can happen down the street from the brewery.

The most important thing we do to guarantee freshness—and something Paul does as well—is to show open dating on our products. I may piss people off by saying this, but I believe that there's no excuse for anyone who cares about the quality of their beer to hide the date it was packaged by using funny codes and illegible numbers. It's no harder to print your labels showing the months in plain English and then notch the month when the beer goes bad, than it is to notch a funny code. All you do when you hide the freshness date is to give yourself the ability to sell stale beer—and also give that ability to retailers and wholesalers who don't care. But when you put open dating on the product, you take that ability away from them. All of a sudden, the beer's freshness is no secret. The consumer knows it, the retailer knows it, and the wholesaler's salesperson knows it. You've won two-thirds of the battle for freshness when you've done that. But it does mean you will have to take back stale beer and absorb the product loss.

Beyond putting the freshness date on each bottle or case of

beer, we put our own salespeople in each of the markets. Nationwide, we have about fifty salespeople who are in the wholesalers' warehouses all the time, checking our beer's date. It's at the wholesalers and retailers that your beer goes bad. The wholesaler puts five pallets of your beer behind the Miller Lite and three months later, your beer is stale. You have to check the wholesalers' warehouses pretty regularly, but you're never going to have 100 percent of your beer fresh. You have to accept that fact. What you have to do is work constantly to make sure as little as possible goes out-of-date. With fifty salespeople, we can survey each of the markets on a weekly basis, and right now, about one out of 700 bottles of Samuel Adams is more than four months old. That's better than it has ever been. Also, doing more volume gives us faster turnover and ensures that our beer is fresher.

Question: *Jim, how much product loss do you have?*

Jim Koch: The big issue is out-of-date beer, and we have about 4,000 cases a year of that. But we can always find a good use for beer. We recently held a great event in Boston. We had 1,200 cases of out-of-date beer we had collected over the year, and we needed to open the bottles so we could refill them. We had a bottle opening contest for all the bartenders in Boston. The winner won a trip to the Great American Beer Festival. We got all the bottles open and then poured the beer into a big dunking tank. The tank held 900 gallons of beer, and I sat on top of it, suit and all, until I got dunked.

Question: *When you open a market, what do you look for?*

Jim Koch: Basically you look for markets where there's a lot of imported beer being sold. We have spread out geographically based on that factor.

Paul Shipman: I think it's apparent in this industry that we compete with foreign beers—with off-shore beer manufacturers. But when your brewery attains a critical mass and a presense in its community and its market, you begin to attract consumers who weren't buying Heineken or Corona. In fact, you give them the opportunity to look at a microbrewed beer as a completely new thing, not as a simple replacement for foreign beer. You begin to supplant foreign beer and build a new consumer franchise, a niche.

We clearly see that in our market. We subdivided Seattle by neighborhoods and could see different patterns in different neighborhoods. There were areas in the northend of Seattle that didn't have much consumption of imported beer, but through a combination of promotion and building up awareness in the taverns, beer and wine bars, we created a consumer awareness for our beer. The objective of any business is actually to create customers, not merely take someone else's, although you have to start somewhere. If you can create customers, then the potential for the industry is bigger than the $1 billion import business in the U.S. today; it's an increasing part of the country's $18 billion beer business.

Question: *Paul, how much did it cost you to get your neon sign on the Northern Exposure television show?*

Paul Shipman: Here's what happened: The people from Northern Exposure called us up and said they were making an initial summer run of the series. They needed a bar in the script, but the bar had to have signage. They didn't have the budget to concoct brands, and the (producers) in New York told them they couldn't have national brands. So they asked us, along with the other microbrewers in the Northwest. We all faxed them our logos and they faxed them to the people in New York. The people in New York said, "There's no way that these things really exist, so go ahead and use them."

We didn't charge them for using our sign. Instead, we had a

party for them, and that's why we had the prime space.

Question: *Gentlemen, how can you figure out the demographics of your customers, and if you were going to buy radio time, what type of station would you choose?*
Jim Koch: Just go look into bars and see who's drinking your beer. That's the best way I know. It's tricky because our customers cut across a lot of traditional demographics. We get fifty-, sixty-, seventy-year-old people who remember what beer used to taste like. We get a lot of women who got tired of drinking Chablis. It's pretty tricky to find a common demographic, unlike for imports where the men are twenty to forty. We've advertised on some classical music stations.

Paul Shipman: We don't advertise, so we've never had to deal with that. I think it's easy to get hung up on who your customers are and lose track of a very simple thing: your customers are people who love good beer. If you start putting any greater limitations on them—they have to be rich, they have to be white, they have to be yuppies, or they have to have a certain type of attitude and lifestyle—you eliminate potential customers. You have to be able to go where beer is being consumed. You have to go with a mission that you're making a superior product and that people are entitled to the opportunity to have better beer. So your mission becomes one of improving the quality of life in our country.

Question: *What kind of events have you sponsored ways to educate people about different types of beers?*
Paul Shipman: We are not big on the sponsorship. Basically, we're pretty stingy when it comes to marketing. However, we do like the romance of beer. We have found that if you can get the full attention of one or two salespeople in a distributorship, and get

them to preach the gospel of your beer, then you've pretty much accomplished your mission. You can't hope to get the whole group. If you get one or two leaders, pretty soon they'll teach the others.

We're publicity conscious and try to structure events. We use the brewery as a communication vehicle. We have tours of the brewery. We have a pub at the brewery that is the inner-sanctum of beer drinking in Seattle. That's our way of doing it.

Jim Koch: I feel pretty much the way Paul does. You've got to be real stingy about those kinds of things. We get one or two requests a week; they all have good reasons and they all want our money. Our philosophy is, we provide them with beer—draft since the costs are lower. But give them money? Not very often.

Question: *How about educating your sales force about beer?*

Jim Koch: That's very important because our sales force is how we communicate with the retailers. Every new salesperson works at the brewery for a couple of days. They are quizzed about their knowledge of beer based on books, mostly by Michael Jackson. Every new salesperson goes to the Great American Beer Festival and once a year, we hold a training session where we walk them through the brewing process, describe the different beers and train them to recognize oxidized beer and various undesireable fermentation byproducts, which are the main problems on the market.

They are also trained to give a thirty-minute seminar to the staff of restaurants. That's really important and is something I learned from Matthew Reich of New Amsterdam Brewing. Each of our salespeople has a kit containing jars of malt, hops and other brewing materials. Retailers want something different at their staff meetings so we come in and give their people a beer class and a t-shirt when it's legal to do so. In the course of a year, we do 2,500 of those all over the country. Maybe we get fifteen people per tasting, so for what it's worth, we're getting 30,000 or 40,000 servers a year who know something about beer.

Question: *How do you establish territories for your salespeople? Does a typical salesperson handle "x" number of accounts or "x" number of square miles?*
Jim Koch: There are no hard-and-fast rules. As a rough idea, someone can handle a market in Minneapolis, Dallas, Atlanta, or Miami. As for the extremes, our person in Seattle handles everything from Oregon to North Dakota and up to Alaska. He's got 30 percent of the land mass in the U.S. On the other extreme, the salesperson in New York City handles half of the East Side.

At some point salespeople begin to handle wholesalers instead of accounts. It really depends on the geography. One person might have forty wholesalers. A person can handle about 120 accounts. It's tough to make more than fifteen to twenty calls a day to retailers and still have any quality.

Paul Shipman: Sales force management has an alchemy of its own. It's different for everybody.

Question: *What kind of incentives can you offer retailers?*
Jim: You can say, "Thank you, you've done a good job." There is a federal law and a lot of state laws against a brewery giving any inducement to a retailer. In a lot of states, just buying retailers lunch can get you into trouble. Every state is different. One salesman for Boston Beer Company lost his license in Texas for two weeks because he mentioned to a retailer the name of a printer who could print our menu cards. Even that was illegal.

Question: *How much confidence do you place in the future of the microbrewing and brewpub movement in the U.S.? What is your gut feeling? People say it's going to grow to 400 or 500 brewpubs.*

Jim Koch: Your guess is as good as mine. I think we're still sailing in turbulent waters here. My gut feeling is that brewpubs will probably do quite well, but microbrewering is a different business and the economies of scale can be pretty brutal. Certainly the financial track record of microbreweries has not been all that great. There are a few success stories, and there are other people who have lost millions of dollars. I think it's hard to predict.

Paul Shipman: I see a very positive picture for microbreweries and brewpubs in the U.S. and domestically-produced specialty beer in general. The limiting factors are the quality of the suppliers, the nature of the resources available for technical assistance, and the financing.

The ability of these businesses to get financing is very, very important. From the late 1960s to the early 1980s, there was a period of rapid growth in the premium wine business, the industry I was in before I got into the specialty beer business. That was a period when there was investment tax credit, rapid depreciation, relatively free-and-easy access to capital, and a lot of inflation. Look what happened: wine is a real industry.

Microbreweries came in during the middle of the 1980s—a far more difficult period in the economic life of the U.S. in which to launch an industry. Yet I am confident—and I believed this even in 1981—that there is no reason to import beer into a country with an industrial economy. That just doesn't make sense. This country still imports beer valued roughly at $1 billion dollars a year. That practice is destined to disappear. The forces of history will cause it to fade out. So an important part of our mission is to supplant that business. If that is the case, everyone in this room can be a millionaire.

Question: *Paul, do you see the major breweries being able to successfully produce specialty beer?*

Paul Shipman: Here's my scenerio on any major brewery launching an all-malt, specialty beer brand—a high-flavor, high-profile beer like we produce. If they do it enough times, they will manage to get one out of the test market. Then when they manage to get it into some form of national distribution, they will go through the whole process of saying, "Well, it just doesn't register on the Richter scale of market share. Maybe if we just make it a little bit lighter, we can open up some new customers for it." Then they will start the process of lightening it. Budweiser, which is a tremendously successful beer and is an important beer on a global basis—which could well be "the world beer"—it started out as a beer that could be served side-by-side with Samuel Adams or Redhook. No, I don't see a problem with the big guys. That's the least of our problems.

Question: *But is there enough room on the retailers' shelves for every beer?*

Jim Koch: It seems to me that as people wake up to beer, they are going to discover that beer has all the enormous variety and complexity of wine. You see zillions of wines, and it wouldn't surprise me, as people really begin to appreciate beer, to see the same kind of complexity in beer. People have already learned that there's more to life than Bud. I think that once a grand proliferation begins, it doesn't stop. Instead, what's going to happen is that whole chunks of brands are going to disappear. Until now, there has always been a brewery that would pick up a troubled brand. That's one reason there haven't been a lot of bankruptcies; somebody would always pick up the pieces. But now, with the Heileman bankruptcy in progress, there's nobody to do that. And retailers are beginning to cull their import beer sections so there's not so much duplication. That should open up several more feet of retail shelf space.

Question: *What do you think about adding brands to your product line?*

Jim Koch: My guess is that if you do it judiciously, it will probably increase your total sales. There is some cannibalization, but you also pick up additional consumers. Anyway, you get tired of making and selling the same beers all the time. It's just fun to make different things. We tried a Cranberry Lambic, but we just couldn't sell it outside of about six bars in the world. We couldn't even sell it in Seattle; it was just too strange. But different beers are fun to do and even though they have no economic justification at all, they're part of what we're all about.

Paul Shipman: There's one special item I think is critical and absolutely, postively must exist in every specialty brewery, and that's Christmas beer. That's the one beer that really does translate into additional business. It's also a great way to position your whole company as doing something special. And the elegance of it is that you stop making it. If you have a small brand, you have to maintain it and nurture it, and that's where the problem lies.

Question: *Can you comment on how you feel the anti-alcohol movement affects you?*

Jim Koch: I find it a very scary thing. I think long-term, it could stigmatize alcohol consumption, almost like cigarettes are being stigmatized. My family has made alcohol for 150 years, and there's no two ways about it—we have made alcohol. It happened to be in the form of beer, but it was alcohol and it was for people to enjoy. I've always felt very good about what I do. I think we all should. We're lucky enough to make a product that not only has a lot of tradition and history, but it's something that enriches peoples lives. If alcohol is a drug, it's a miracle drug. Research shows that two bottles of beer a day will cut your heart attack risk by 30 percent; that's a miracle. But unfortunately, the law does not allow brewers to talk about the therapeutic value of their product. I can't copy the *New York Times* article about that study and send it out to customers because that would be illegal. That's a very scary thing to me. My sense is, in the next five or ten years, we microbrewers will be the beneficiaries of neoprohibition because as people drink less, they drink better. I guess I have a very long-term view of this business. It probably won't hurt me, but it may hurt my son.

Paul Shipman: Prohibition is a peculiarly American concern, but I think it's a trend that has served us in the past. When people start talking about neoprohibition a lot—not just in the industry but in the world at large—and it creeps into the collective conversation, people will start asking themselves just how bad alcohol can be. The other American phenomenon is a fundamental distrust of authority that will work to our benefit, so I'm not too uptight about this one. I believe the crescendo of anti-alcohol sentiment may already have passed. I think it's possible that we are on the downslope of it.

Question: *Another problem looming over the microbrewing industry might be the duration of the tax exemption for small breweries. Do you think that as mircobreweries begin to proliferate the exemption will be revoked?*
Paul Shipman: Well, that exemption is such a wonderful thing. If you believe it is going to go on forever just the way it is, you're just a little bit too optimistic. I'm inherently an optimistic person, and I believe it won't be fully taken away, but it may be watered down. I think in a couple years we'll say, "Hey, 60,000 barrels,

that's too small, that's discriminatory. Let's get it up to 100,000 barrels."

Question: *Will you comment on where you spend your advertising dollars most effectively, whether it's magazine or newspaper?*
Jim Koch: Point of sale.

Paul Shipman: Point of sale. The only other place to invest is in the publicity: telecommunications, press releases and events that are structured for media attention. My view about media advertising is that it is supposed to make the whole thing easy. But it's not that easy, and it's only through promotional events that require hardwork and creativity, that we build value. We have to be creative. It helps our industry when we do things that are totally unexpected.

Question: *What kind of relationship have you had with your bankers?*
Paul Shipman: The banking environment is bad coast-to-coast; however, the banks are getting behind a few of their customers that they expect to be around for awhile. We have always had good relations with the bank. Our financial officer David Michaelson is in charge of that. That's not a problem right now. but it's important to cultivate that relationship.

Jim Koch founded the Boston Beer Company in 1984.
Paul Shipman founded the Redhook Ale Brewery of Seattle in 1982.

Chapter 15.

STRATEGIC MARKET PLANNING

*Daniel Bradford,
Boulder, Colorado*

Strategic market planning, long the sole provenance of large corporations, is filtering down to small companies. While the advent of the personal computer has helped to affect this change, the spread of sound business knowledge cannot be overlooked as a factor. More and more companies are adopting strategic market planning as a means of achieving measurable results, reaching desired goals, and bringing order into the seemingly chaotic process of selling.

Confusion may cloud the distinction between strategic marketing plans and business plans. While many find it difficult to separate the two, it is useful to think of the business plan as the overall operations of the company and the marketing plan as the means to reach the consumer.

A strategic market plan has three components. First, it is a strategy, the game plan by which a company intends to achieve its stated objectives. Second, its concern is the market, as it is focused on the consumer and how the company can gain their participation. Third, it is a plan that lays out the steps by which a company can move through its marketing program and assess the results.

Why Devise a Plan?

Most people are critical of strategic marketing planning. They find that it takes too much time to do and the information required is too difficult to uncover. They would rather rely on their direct experience of the industry and loosely derived objectives to guide their business.

Before discounting a plan, however, you really need to examine the goals and objectives of your company and the pressures of succeeding in a highly competitive industry. The axiom of not being able to hit a target if you don't have one is not only appropriate, but it is very poignant. Often the target may be exclusively a certain sales volume or a certain profit margin, and thus embody the simple approach to goal setting.

Both of these end results could disguise either weaknesses or strengths that are being overlooked. The purpose of a plan is to reveal information in both of these areas, provide a calculated method of examining them, and set measures to evaluate success or failure, weaknesses and strengths.

I have watched an association implement a strategic marketing plan as the primary method of gaining control of its spiraling growth, maximize the value of marketing dollars, and decide on directions to take and those to avoid. Besides relieving a measure of anxiety, the plan provided a back drop for decision-making. It is now part of the association's annual program.

How to Make a Plan

Creating a strategic marketing plan can appear to be overwhelming; however, the key players are already on hand and the data readily available. And the time-line can be very specific.

Senior management are the only people with the complete overview of the company. They have the ability to paint a broad picture. Yet, they are more often than not too close to the material to render an objective opinion. They need to direct the project, provide meaningful data and evaluate the results.

Consultants are useful in that they have an ability to structure a plan and contend with each component separately. As outsiders, they are less likely to deal with internal issues that may stand in the way of a neutral and effective plan.

Staff and other people in the production and distribution channels have hands-on information derived from experience. They have formulated opinions from their on-going involvement and may have input that can be significant. From secretaries to distributors, players in a company have impressions, gossip, hard information, and suggestions that are of value to the plan.

Beyond the people within an organization's structure there are numerous published sources of information. From trade magazines to industry associations, there is a wealth of data available at a nominal cost. In the small brewery industry, with its local and regional markets and its ground-breaking attitudes, many of the participants are quite willing to provide supporting data to new entrants, especially from noncontiguous markets.

A four-month time-line is typical for a complete strategic marketing plan. This normally proceeds in four stages. First is the task description with the segments and resources laid out clearly. Second is the first draft derived from the analysis of information. The third stage is the review of the document by key members in the organization. The fourth stage is submission of the completed document and its implementation.

The time-frame for the strategic marketing plan reflects the corporate objectives. Five-year plans are becoming common, with quarterly reviews typical for most industries. I work with a restaurant that produces quarterly objectives and plans that are seasonal increments of their annual plan. After the first year, the process takes less than a week each quarter to complete.

The following sections outline each of the segments of a complete strategic marketing plan. I have tried to present the value of each section and what to look for in that section. Collecting the appropriate information can lead to sound business decisions that will chart the course of the company.

Corporate Philosophy

The beginning is the corporate philosophy or mission statement. This is the basis against which all objectives are measured. Succinctly stated, it is the heart of the company. In the new brewer industry, participants may state a desire for a certain quality atmosphere in a brewpub or a certain level of product excellence in a microbrewery. However, what is often lacking in a mission statement is the scope of activities, the quality of environment for the employees and the community interaction—all of which add depth to the mission statement. How do you want to grow? Who do you want to bring into your consumer group? What working environment are you seeking?

Corporate Objectives

Too often the corporate objectives are stated in hard-and-fast percentage growth figures, such as 15 percent, or in a slogan, such as "brew the best beer in the state." Both methods suffer from ambiguity and a lack of understanding of the potentials in the products and the market. Rather, corporate objectives should be based on available information and resources brought to bear on the uniqueness of the business.

For example, I worked with one client who, based on historical data and new forces in the market, projected a healthy growth rate for one product line. He saw the introduction of numerous, noncompetitive products in another line and projected a significantly higher growth rate than previous years for that line. He speculated that external risks would keep another product line at the same rate as before. The fourth product line had too many organizational problems so he estimated slightly less growth than the previous year. Overall he was almost exactly on target.

Analysis of External Environment

The analysis of external factors should take into account the social, economic and political environment and best guesses about their effect on the conduct of business. Projected over a five-year period, these influences can be quite telling.

For our industry external factors are becoming critical. With neoprohibitionism on the rise, and the similar efforts to restrict marketing and increase taxes, today's brewers need to clearly understand the forces at work that will affect their efforts. In addition, the consumption of alcoholic beverages, on a per captia basis, is declining. Furthermore, international trading issues may have a direct affect on the strength of the industry. Consolidation among distributors, the slow withering of old regional breweries, the rise of new specialty distributors, and the increase of new regionals provide cross-currents for our business. Demographic trends are pointing to less mobility and disposable income and more sedentary, at-home, family lifestyles.

Internal Organization

The internal organization can dictate the quality and efficiency of the marketing campaign. One of the critical issues for most corporations is the preponderate influence of the desire to get a quality product to the market. An examination of internal organizations often reveal an acceptable rift between production and marketing. Marketing is the whole business seen from the point of view of the customer. Production creates the quality product that the customer wants.

Given this definition, the internal organization needs to reflect not only the objective of creating the appropriate product, but also the whole process of involvement with the consumer. A successful marketing plan helps guide the organizational structure into bringing product, packaging, research, publicity, advertising, and promotion to the sales program. Who collects data? Who overseas merchandise? Who participates in territory decisions? Whose responsibility is it too decide on menu changes?

Competitive Analysis

The competitive analysis is second nature to the business owner. Watching the trends in the industry, variances and consistency in sales, structural changes, and new successes are all the hallmark of a successful business owner. Bringing them together into a useful statement of the competition often is overlooked in the haste to sell the product.

With such a changing industry, restaurants, bars and packaged beers, a competitive analysis can reveal budding weaknesses and emerging opportunities. High-end restaurants are closing. Does that mean there is room for neighborhood bars? Exchange rates are cutting into import sales. Does that provide more shelf space for new beers? Brand leaders are falling off. Is the consumer tired of their products?

Market Potential Analysis

The analysis of the market potential of a product often takes second status to the dreams of the company head. Personal experiences and other companies' successes often can lead to unrealistic and dangerous projections.

The first step is identifying the niche for the products. The new brewer industry is so well established that the niche paths have already been laid out. A tour of a new market will reveal the other contenders and the depth of their penetration. A few calls to different distributors can often uncover the scale of that penetration. Examining the bars and restaurants can uncover weaknesses in product placement or an opportunity for a brewpub. Data from the beer industry, facts from distributors and license holders and personal experience can combine to provide hard facts about a new territory. Rigorous analysis is needed to understand the degree of saturation and the competitive opportunities.

Market Share Analysis

The degree of saturation, or market-share analysis, reveals the opportunities in a new territory. Market-share analysis continues along both company and product segment. Inconsistent domination by a single company uncovers both market acceptance of a product and opportunities for bridgeheads. A scattering of similar products from a variety of sources suggests possibilities for either room for a new entrant or a weak player that could be replaced.

The critical aspect of market-share analysis is found in the changing nature of the new brewing industry. On the one hand, beers are often identified by the brewer, the microbrewer niche. Still with acceptance of new beers, beer-style niches are creating new opportunities; witness the success of wheat beers.

I presently have a ring-side seat for two separate market share challenges affecting the same client. A competitor is moving in on his territory believing that either there are enough clients to go around or that the clients are ripe for theft. Simultaneously in another market, my client is going up against an established institution believing that there is another niche of prospects not touched by that business.

Product-Line Analysis

Product-line segmentation is one of the standard methods of

growth for businesses. However, prior to expansion, existing lines must be fully examined. Whether a line is fully established, peaked and stabilized, or being bypassed by newer lines must be explored. Watching the trends in others' product sales, whether they are sudden winners, losers or slow to penetrate, can uncover the patchwork of product lines that spell success.

Within the examination of product lines are the statistical problems of evaluation. Gross revenues or units such as cases can give interesting materials, but if the margins differ dramatically from one line to another, the comparison is of little value.

I watched one brewer pin his company to the belief that a product line exists between microbrewed products and major brewed products. His product-line analysis suggested that there was a niche between the fuller products of the new brewers and the lighter more common beers. The jury is still out on his analysis.

Customer Client Analysis

Customer client analysis is always difficult for the small business. Without big budgets for research, small business owners are often left with guesswork. However, having worked on large research projects with powerful statistical tools, I have not been too impressed with their ability to really define their customer in a meaningful way. I enjoy telling people about the 45 percent female attendance at the Great American Beer Festival. Yet, all the female attendees I have spoken with report that their reason for attending is to meet men and not because of the beer.

Still, it is imperative to develop an understanding of the demographic and psychographic attributes of the targeted customer. This industry has become enamored of the yuppie profile—the imported beer drinker. This leaves out the passionate loyalty of college students, the nostalgic tastes of older Europeans, and the enduring support of the blue-collar worker who likes full flavor.

Standing outside a retailer cooler or wandering from bar to bar is a start on market research. Stopping to talk with your customers or route drivers can also lead to usable conclusions. Creating your own mailing list through cards dropped in a bowl at the bar or coupons or premiums will give you people to survey.

Pricing Analysis

For the seasoned brewer, pricing analysis is old hat. Pricing is well accepted as the single most important marketing tool for consumer products. It defines the niche, the number of turns, the outlets, and the handling of a product. Many negotiations with retail outlets begin with the price points for the product.

However, a successful pricing analysis has to include several factors. First and foremost, does the price point support the objectives of the company? A lower price point can stimulate sales, but if handled incorrectly, it can stigmatize the product. A lower price point may be required in order to get established, with increases anticipated in the future. Still, the clients attracted to that point may not stay with the increase. Geographical and outlet variances in price pointing have to be part of the plan.

Channels of Distribution

Channels of distribution are the various ways of bringing a product to market. Direct sales, commission reps, warehouse outlets, and distributors are a few of the popular channels. The particular channels used directly affects the success of reaching the particular customer. With the beer industry, there are very few different opportunities. The most overlooked aspect of planning the channels of distribution is the fact that distribution costs a fixed rate. Regardless of the method, the costs are still there, and they invariably work out to be the same regardless.

The distributor is at the apex for the beer industry. The type of distributor chosen is a strategic marketing question, as is the product selection offered. However, the new brewer movement and the consolidation of the distributing industry have created different possibilities. Self-distribution and brewpubs are opening up new distribution channels, and young, specialty houses have taken a new approach to beer sales.

Marketing Personnel Analysis

Marketing personnel analysis has three aspects. The first addresses the implementation of the strategic marketing plan; who will oversee the implementation? Second is the data gathering; where will the facts come from and who will present them? Third is the sales force; who in the field will follow through?

While all three functions too often fall on the shoulders of the owner, with the expected slippage, it is advisable to consider taking a team approach. Clerical personnel can handle data gathering. Brokers, commissioned sales reps, route drivers, waiters, waitresses are in position to provide an analysis of the execution. The owner operator usually stays in the directors seat.

However, there are consultants and agencies who can take on this work and may—factoring in labor, overhead, taxes, etc.—be as cost effective in managing the service account as the owner/operator would be. Be advised that taking this approach could lead to a whole other series of headaches.

Marketing Budget

The marketing budget is its own strategic weapon. Its size can reflect industry standard, it can reflect the life cycle of a product, it can reflect the short-term strategic objectives, or it can reflect the corporate philosophy. Regardless of the determining factor, the marketing budget should be all-inclusive and specific. It represents the base against which success can be measured.

Marketing budgets vary from industry to industry. Custom homebuilders rarely spend more than 3 percent and restaurants are often closing in on 15 percent. I have heard brewers quote ranges from 13 to 21 percent, wholesale, per case, for marketing costs. However, hard-and-fast ratios miss the concept of a marketing plan established to meet certain sales objectives. High expenses for introductions and low expenses for stagnant brands figure into the budget. Seasonal boosts in promotions and annual cycles suggest more than a linear budget approach. A certain sales volume may require a particularly heavy push, and a certain corporate position could demand expensive art work.

In the new brewer industry, word of mouth and reputation are the stock in trade for success. The high-touch, low-cost approach is most common. Still, the sweat equity that goes into getting this rolling remains a marketing expense.

Marketing Strategies

Marketing strategies are derived from the analysis of the previous subjects. The process is highly reflective as you move between objectives and opportunities, structures and limitations. The conclusion comes as a decision about how you are going to do what you want to. This is when the off-hand statement "I'm going to sell 10,000 cases of beer" becomes the more specific "I have to sell 14,500 cases of beer retailed at $5.99 through specialty houses that compete for bonuses, with a focus on on-premise accounts that are strongly food orientated, supported by the owner in sales and clerical help in data processing, with four-color posters, a rugby team sponsorship, and a graduaal expansion in territory to exceed eighty miles from base."

Marketing Tactics

The challenge here is in creating effective tools that achieve the objectives. The analysis can draw from the company's history and the strategies and tactics used by the competition. In the marketing business, the swipe file—a collection of appealing material stored for a rainy, brain-storm day—is the source of numerous programs. Marketing tactics combine the tried-and-true methods with the innovative. The mix can be culled from traditional strategies such as merchandising, advertising, public relations, special events, and promotions. Within each of these strategies are tactics that are consistent with the corporate philosophy, brands, competition, channels of distribution, and geographic market.

This is most often "subed" out to creative individuals or agencies. Having the talent match the company, making sure that all the points of contact with the customer are consistent, and staying on schedule are key issues for the strategic planner.

Marketing Activities Time-table

Most companies often fail to devise the time-table for their marketing activities. Yet, the time-table defines the tasks and objectives that inform the effort. Historical data can lay a firm foundation for the time-table. Parceling out the objectives by quarter, based on past years activity, can delineate the marketing activity required to meet those activities. Planning out the preparation steps for each activity creates the task charts for the personnel concerned, giving each a concrete goal.

In my years of work with a custom-home builder, I was able to help him define the sales objectives by his typical seasonal activity, factoring in the two home shows that always provide a boost in sales. We could take this schedule and allocate the advertising, commissions, public relations, and brochure costs and schedules. With this time-table, we were able to gang several print and advertising productions thus reducing costs, sustaining marketing flexibility, and maintaining a consistent public image.

Reviews and Evaluation

At the end of the school term come the report cards. After decades of public school, people are used to a literal evaluation. In a business, this comes from a look at the bottom line. Is there a profit? Were enough barrels sold? Was the projected growth achieved? These sorts of figures, while often providing profound elation or deep depression, often disguise the true success or failure. The key to strategic marketing lies in reaching consumers.

Each of the above sections has its own measure of success or failure, beginning with the corporate philosophy. Was profitability achieved at the price of a devalued public image? Have the objectives failed to take advantage of the potential or are they taxing the limits of the company? What about staff morale? Are they creating more customers or turning them aside? Have the channels of distribution led to smooth delivery of the product is the consumer confused by empty shelves or spoiled product that typifies your brands? Has the industry moved away from the price points? Are the marketing materials going unused or hitting at the wrong time? Were the deadlines met? Did the budget work?

Conclusion

Even for the adventuresome traveler, it is often better to have a map. It also is prudent to know the lay of the land. The same holds true for the small business owner. Professional responsibility alone commends the creation of a strategic marketing plan. A good plan shows you where to go, how to get there, and provides the resources to determine whether you arrived at all.

Since 1981, Daniel Bradford has been the director of The Great American Beer Festival, the largest American beer fest. He has been a marketing consultant for ten years specializing in brewery/restaurants.

Chapter 16.

ACHIEVING STABILITY USING MEMBRANE FILTRATION

Peter Meier,
Millipore Corporation

Membrane filtration is the premier method of achieving microbiological stability in the bottle. No chemicals and, perhaps more importantly, no heating is required. The organoleptic properties are preserved in a completely natural state until the product is opened, be it weeks or months after filling.

Successful aseptic filling (*aseptic* meaning preventing infection and also free from undesirable microorganisms) requires a "sanitary mind set." Factors that bear on this include the location, sizing, design, operation, and monitoring of the entire system. The up-stream fining and clarifying steps, the membranes that actually remove the microbes, the filling operation, the bottles, and the closures are all important aspects. Also, the plumbing, auxiliary fluids (such as counterpressure gases) to the filler, containers, and all associated equipment require close adherence to standard sanitizing procedures and careful monitoring.

For over two decades, large and small bottlers of beer, wine, coolers, and juices have used membrane filtration as a part of their aseptic filling system. During this time, there have evolved several rules and guidelines for success, which I shall discuss.

Membrane Filters

A membrane filter is a thin (0.1 mm) sheet of polymeric film with carefully controlled porosity (percent void volume) and pore dimensions. Polyvinylidene fluoride, nylon and cellulose esters are among the plastic materials from which membranes are made. Membrane filters retain microorganisms predominantly by a sieving action. Common pore size ratings are 0.22, 0.45, 0.65, 0.8, and 1.2 micrometers (hereafter called *microns*).

These ratings were established according to the membrane's microbial retention performance. Thus, 0.22 micron membranes quantitatively retain very small bacteria like *Pseudomonas diminuta*, and 0.45 micron membranes quantitatively retain slightly larger bacteria such as *Lactobacillus brevis*. Quantitative retention usually implies at least 10^9 or 99.9999999 percent reduction in the concentration of microbes downstream of the membrane.

Membrane filters are commonly supplied as cartridge elements in lengths from ten to forty inches. Each ten-inch cartridge or the equivalent usually contains from five-to-eight square feet of surface area in a pleated configuration. The flow is from outside to inside, and the filtered beverage exits the cartridge through the open-ended throat, which is secured into a housing with one or more o-rings or gaskets.

Although the cartridge style is the most common configuration, flat sheets of membrane and newer small devices like stacked-disk units are also available.

Because some spoilage organisms are smaller than one micron, for example, lactic-acid bacteria, most beer bottlers choose a final filter with a rated pore size of 0.45 microns. Larger pore sizes give higher throughputs, but they do not match the bacterial retention properties of a 0.45 micron membrane. A more open-pore size would be chosen only to ensure retention of spoilage yeasts and molds (not all bacteria) or to achieve a high degree of clarity.

Although membrane filters have relatively low "dirt-holding" capacity and are more expensive than pads or prefilters, their performance justifies their cost. Since the pore structure of a membrane guarantees absolute hold-back of undesired particles or microorganisms, it can be regarded as an insurance policy for the user.

One way to keep costs down is to be sure that the beverage introduced into a membrane filter is reasonably free of plugging contaminants and microorganisms. Even though a beverage may have sparkling clarity, it can plug a tight membrane quickly if it contains colloidal carbohydrates, for example. Pretreatment is accomplished by up-stream fining operations, and by pad and/or diatomaceous earth (DE) filtration.

Sometimes, a special set of cartridge filters (commonly known as *prefilters*) are used just before the final membrane. Prefilters often have nominal or approximate pore size ratings and are placed immediately upstream of the final membrane to remove any remaining colloids. The nominal ratings for prefilter cartridges are usually much closer to absolute ratings than are the nominal ratings for DE and inexpensive depth filters, i.e., some pads or string-wound or molded cartridges. Prefilters are carefully selected and tested by the supplier to improve the overall economy of the process. Suppliers of membrane filters usually recommend methods to test the "filterability" or the expected membrane throughput of the beverage. A "filterability" test can often identify a beverage containing an excess of plugging constituents. Additional upstream treatments, such as fining or tighter prefiltration, may greatly improve filter throughputs and hence overall economy. If such tests show the presence of colloids which may prematurely plug final membranes, a prefilter or a very tight pad is the best choice.

Sizing

Because membrane filters offer a fairly high resistance to flow, differential pressure is an important sizing consideration for both final membrane and prefilter cartridges. Also, the rate at which membranes plug is always dependent upon "face velocity." This is the rate of flow per unit area of filtration media. The greater the face velocity, the faster the plugging.

To understand the effect of face velocity, visualize pouring rice through a coarse sieve. At a rapid flow, the kernels may bridge the openings and prevent passage. At a slower face velocity, the kernels do not bridge, but flow cleanly through the openings. (This is not to infer that slower flow rates allow microorganisms to pass through. The pore size of a final membrane filter prevents larger particles, including organisms, from penetrating the membrane's surface at any face velocity.)

A good rule of thumb for final membrane filters is to stay below 0.50 gallon/minute per square foot of final membrane area. Thus, if the maximum demand of your filler is ten gallons/minute, you need at least twenty square feet of membrane area. At this face velocity, the pressure drop at startup is usually 2 psi or less across the membrane.

For most depth media, including some cartridge prefilters, a similar rule of thumb is 0.16 to 0.25 gallon/minute per square foot of medium. Therefore, the area of pretreatment medium should be sized at two or three times the final membrane area. Proper filter area sizing gives both low startup pressure drops and the most economical filtration costs.

If the annual cost of the cartridges approaches the initial capital investment for housings and associated hardware, lower face velocities, i.e., a larger membrane area, should be considered. Within a short time, the savings in the disposables will more than offset the investment in larger housings to hold additional membranes and prefilters.

When sizing a system, there are two other important considerations. The first is the pump or pressure source. For example, if your supplier recommends running the filters (pre- and final) up to a differential pressure of 30 psi each, and your filler requires 20 psi operating pressure, this means that a pumping capacity of 80 psi (30+30+20) at the filler's demand flow is required in order to continue if both filters are nearly plugged. Filling with only tank head pressure or with an undersized pump will limit filter throughput by forcing shutdown before acceptable pressure drops have been reached, i.e., before the cartridges are truly plugged.

The second consideration involves sizing a system for throughput. Filler downtime for a large bottler can be very expensive. If the bottling schedule or beverage variability, i.e., use of the same filters for different beverages, results in unplanned downtime, it may be prudent to install duplicate filtration trains (have the second set-up ready to go if the first one plugs). Alternatively, the system should be sized large enough to ensure completion of a given batch with plenty of margin for plugging.

Design

Several important rules must be followed when designing a filtration system:

1. The final membrane must be housed in equipment designed to minimize both holdup and stagnant areas where microorganisms can grow. There must be no dead ends that cannot be easily sanitized.

2. Sanitary plumbing including piping, pressure gauges, valves, and connections must be used for all lines downstream of the final filter.

3. There should be a minimum length of downstream piping

and fittings. Pumps should never be placed between the final filter and the filler.

4. Hoses, plastics, and non-polished metals cannot be sanitized easily. Therefore, the final filter housings and all downstream plumbing should be polished stainless steel of grades 304 or 316.

5. Locate valves for sanitary sampling at strategic locations to monitor microbiological counts during filling. These locations should be at points upstream of the filters, between the prefilter and the final filter, and immediately downstream of the final filter.

6. Include connections for hot water or steam used to sanitize the system, and for the introduction of pressurized gas to measure filter integrity.

7. Position pressure gauges to monitor the pressure drop (hence plugging rate) of each set of cartridges. It is standard procedure to put pressure gauges immediately upstream and downstream of each housing. If they are downstream of the final filter, the gauge and connections must be of sanitary design.

8. Pressure relief valves should be included upstream of both prefilters and final filters if the pump can exceed the pressure ratings of the housings. These valves also act as vents to permit the escape of entrapped air from the housings (and are commonly located on the top of the housings themselves).

9. Locate the prefilter and final-filter housings adjacent to each other so that the prefilter effluent immediately enters the final-filter housing.

There is one very good reason for this last proximity requirement; submicron filtration removes many "protective" colloids, and molecular rearrangements can cause new colloidal aggregates to form soon after filtration, sometimes within minutes. The best examples are the highly-branched beta-glucan molecules that can form loose but gummy molecular aggregates with proteins. A tight prefiltration breaks up some of the aggregates, but they can reform again within minutes and plug the final filter. Thus, if final membrane filtration follows tight prefiltration and interim storage, the final membrane may become plugged prematurely from new colloids or precipitates induced by the prefilter's clarification and formed during storage.

This same phenomenon is responsible for the occasional clouds, hazes or precipitates that may appear in the bottle even though the beverage has perfect microbiological stability and was of high optical clarity when it was bottled. Examples of these precipitates are proteins, protein-tannin complexes (chillhazes) and tartrates. If a haze or precipitate forms after submicron filtration, additional upstream fining or filtration, enzyme treatment or cold stabilization may be needed prior to final membrane filtration.

Sanitation

Sanitizing the filters and filling/closure equipment prevents microorganisms from contaminating the beverage after filtration. The source(s) of contamination can be either external or from within the system. The best approach is to begin "thinking sanitary" well upstream of the filter. If the tanks, plumbing and equipment are routinely cleaned and sanitized, the microbiological counts in the beverage arriving at the final filters will be under control.

Many breweries are exemplary in this matter, and the numbers of microorganisms at all stages of the process are very low. The final membranes are not heavily burdened, and the achievement of a sterile package is more certain. Yet, though the filtrate from the final filter housing is completely free of microbes, this is no guarantee that organisms cannot enter the beverage from contaminated plumbing, filler spouts, containers, closures, the air around the filler, or the hands of bottling employees. It is essential that the following occur:

• the entire operation be designed and constructed with atten-

tion to sanitary operation,
- the filling area be located away from possible sources of extraneous contamination,
- the equipment be sanitized routinely,
- equipment, containers and closures be monitored routinely for contamination.

Heat (preferably in the form of hot water) is the most common method used to sanitize a final membrane filter, its housing, the plumbing to the filler, and the filler itself. This is because chemicals, and even gases, penetrate neither the submicron cracks and crevices that may harbor microorganisms nor the biological surface film often found on internal surfaces of piping and other plumbing attachments. Suppliers of aseptic filling equipment usually provide complete instructions for heat sanitation, including the recommended frequency. At a minimum, all components should be sanitized once daily before the start of the filling. Hot water is preferred, but steam is acceptable.

(Note: If steam is used, even more attention to temperature is required. Steam heats by condensing until all surfaces are hot. Only when the temperature of the filler spouts, large metal masses, and gasketing materials reaches the steam's temperature can the sanitation period commence.)

Table 1
Temperature Guidelines for Equipment Sanitation

Temperature	Time
200° F (93° C)	20 minutes
180° F (82° C)	30 minutes
160° F (71° C)	40 minutes
140° F (60° C)	60 minutes

All components from the membranes to the filler spouts must be held at the desired temperature for the suggested time. Temperature-sensitive crayons or other temperature indicators can be used to ensure that the largest metal mass and most remote locations reach the desired temperature. The filler spouts should be open to allow water (or steam) to pass through. **The times in Table 1 do not include the time to reach temperature.**

Use carefully filtered water or steam. Dirty water or steam can plug membrane filters as fast or faster than beverages. Fillers can be sanitized with unfiltered hot water or steam if provisions are made to sanitize the connecting plumbing (a valve) that separates the filler from the filter during this process. It must be noted, however, that unfiltered sanitizing water can leave behind inorganic and organic substances that may accumulate in the filler.

When all components downstream of the final membrane have reached the desired temperature, the hot-water flow may be reduced to maintain the temperature. The lower flow saves energy and reduces filter plugging by colloids in the sanitizing water.

After sanitation, the membrane system is brought back to ambient temperature for the integrity measurement, using cold, filtered water.

The procedure for shutdown (at the end of day) is to chase the remaining beverage with nitrogen, then with cold water, followed by hot water. This flushes the system and may also dissolve colloidal contaminants such as carbohydrates that have collected on the membrane's surfaces.

The sanitation procedure should then be repeated. The filtration system remains sanitary if closed down completely (with valves) overnight or for a weekend.

For long-term storage (more than sixty hours), a sanitizing fluid should be pumped into the system. Acceptable solutions include 0.3 percent peracetic acid, 25 ppm iodoform, 10 ppm chlorine, and metabisulfite at about 500 ppm and pH under 5.0 (Note: *Metabisulfite is corrosive to stainless steel.*)

Integrity Testing

The integrity test is a method used to check whether there are any larger-than-rated pores or leaks in the system through which a microorganism might pass. Each supplier should provide an integrity test procedure to guarantee final membrane performance at the rated pore size. These tests can only be done on absolute media, not on nominally-rated prefilters. Membrane filters should be checked daily before filling to ensure their integrity. The test is done after sanitizing the system. It is good practice to conduct integrity tests at least twice per day, before and after the filling process.

The integrity test measures the passage of gas under controlled conditions through a membrane. There are three popular integrity test methods: bubblepoint, diffusional flow and pressure hold.

Bubblepoint. The most popular integrity test is measurement of the membrane's bubblepoint pressure. Because the pores are small, they can be considered as capillaries that hold liquid against applied gas pressure. When the gas reaches a sufficient pressure to overcome the surface-tension forces, it forces the liquid out of the pores and permits the gas to flow through. Each pore size has a specific gas pressure. The larger the pore, the lower the pressure needed to overcome the surface tension and let the gas pass through.

The membrane must be completely wet with water at ambient temperature before the test is done. Dry pores permit free gas passage. Because the surface tension of water decreases with increased temperature, inaccurate low bubblepoint pressures are measured at higher temperatures. For example, at 140 degrees F compared to 68 degrees F (60 degrees C compared to 20 degrees C), the surface tension of water is lower by almost 10 percent.

A cylinder of nitrogen or compressed air (filtered if possible), a pressure regulator and an accurate pressure gauge (readable to 1 psi increments) are required to do the test. Carbon dioxide cannot be used because of its relatively high solubility in water. Gas is introduced into the system upstream of the membranes. It is first applied at low pressure (about 5 psi) to force the upstream water through the pores of the filter. The bubblepoint pressure is determined by increasing the gas pressure slowly over a period of three-to-five minutes until a continuous flow of **large** bubbles appears downstream.

The bubbles may be observed using an in-line site glass, or a piece of tubing may be aseptically attached downstream of the housing with the other end immersed in a container of clean water to visualize the appearance of the bubbles.

For an 0.45 micron membrane, the bubblepoint is usually greater than 20 psi. If large bubbles appear downstream at a lower pressure than that set by the supplier, the membrane fails integrity.

Diffusional flow. A small stream of very tiny bubbles may appear below the bubblepoint pressure. This is caused by gas molecules dissolving into the water and then diffusing through the wetted membrane matrix. At atmospheric pressure downstream of the membrane, the gas reforms as tiny bubbles. When large membrane areas are used, the diffusional passage of gas may be considerable, and it may be impossible to clearly distinguish between diffusional flow and the bubblepoint.

The diffusional flow integrity test involves measuring this gas diffusion rate at a pressure less than (typically 80 percent of) the bubblepoint pressure. For membrane areas over about 100 square feet, the diffusional test is the most reliable method.

When doing this type of integrity test, an accurate method of measuring gas flow such as a flow meter or a piece of tubing is needed to convey the gas into an inverted water-filled graduated cylinder. The rate of water displacement in the cylinder is the diffusional flow. Manufacturers specify a minimum acceptable diffusional flow rate at (or before) which the membrane's integrity is judged unacceptable.

Pressure hold. The third integrity test is the pressure hold, where the filters are pressurized to a preset level, typically 80 percent of the bubblepoint pressure. The gas supply is then turned off, and integrity is determined by how fast the pressure drops.

A typical specification for acceptance (depending upon the upstream gas volume) may be that the pressure drops no faster than 2 psi in five minutes. A faster drop indicates that openings exist through which the gas can pass, and that these openings are larger than the membrane's rated pore size. This method is similar to the diffusion test, but not as accurate.

Troubleshooting. There may be several reasons why membranes fail the integrity test that are not related to true pore integrity. For instance, the membrane may not be completely wetted, and some of the pores may not be filled with water.

Or sometimes the membrane is not at fault at all; most systems include o-rings or gasket-type seals that may be the cause for integrity failure. However, the net result is the same: the integrity of the system is not sufficient to maintain a microbiologically stable filtrate, and filling should not commence until the problem is found and corrected.

After sanitation, it is possible to visually check the cartridges and seals by removing the bowl (or dome) of the final membrane housing without contaminating the downstream areas. If any seals are interrupted, however, the sanitation procedure must be repeated.

Auxiliary Fluids, Equipment and People

There is no substitute for sanitary operation of the filler and closure equipment. Auxiliary fluids, containers, closures, and people are all possible sources of contamination.

Gases for stirrup-lifting, purging, counterpressure at the filler, conveying, and jetting must be sterile-filtered with membrane filters capable of being sanitized (preferably by steam) and integrity-tested. The plumbing that delivers the fluids, as well as all surfaces with potential fluid or closure contact, must also be kept clean and sanitized regularly.

Any openings between the filter and the filler, such as sampling valves, must be flamed or sprayed with 90 percent isopropanol or 70 percent ethanol before and after opening.

New bottles are usually free of contamination. They should be stored in unopened and undamaged packages or on sealed pallets in a clean, dry area. If exposed to moisture/humidity or if stored for a long time, check for dust, bugs and sterility before use.

Heat sanitation of the filler spouts is the only proven method of ensuring freedom from contamination. This is best accomplished by allowing a trickle flow of hot water through each spout as prescribed in Table 1.

An added insurance during filler downtime is to spray a stream of sanitizing fluid, for example 25 ppm iodoform or 90 percent isopropanol (or 70 percent ethanol) onto each spout. Frequent disassembly and cleaning of each spout, albeit time-consuming, represents the ounce of prevention worth a pound of cure.

Open windows or doors, fans, forklift movement, and bird, rodent or bug droppings can all bring unwanted contamination to the filling and closure areas. All air movement should be controlled by minimizing traffic. The filler and the closure equipment should ideally be isolated to the point of installing clean low ceilings and sidewalls.

Finally, attention paid to the personal hygiene of employees working around the filler, containers, closures, and conveying devices is essential. Operators should wear masks, disposable sterile gloves, clean clothing, and even protective footwear. Once an unwanted organism from any source invades a piece of equipment, the only solution is complete isolation, cleaning and sanitation, and renewed attention to all auxiliary fluids, surfaces, containers, and personnel.

Serial numbering of cases, or at least pallets, allows contaminated product to be identified and isolated, thus avoiding having to scrap the entire lot or the whole day's bottling.

Monitoring

Monitoring the equipment and the product is important to ensure microbiological stability. Sanitary sampling valves should be used to collect in-line product samples. Some suppliers provide kits to monitor the filler spouts, bottles, closures, and even the air around the filler. Swab tests are an easy way to check-up on the efficiency of your sanitation procedures.

To test samples for the absence of spoilage organisms, you need a vacuum source and flasks, petri dishes, lab-sized membranes, nutrient media, an incubator, forceps, a flame burner, and a magnifying viewer or microscope if possible. Samples can be sent out to an outside lab for testing.

Initial, mid-run and end-run product should be sampled, and filler spouts should be monitored daily (or at least weekly). By catching a problem early, it may be remedied so that contaminated product is minimized.

Good housekeeping, strict adherence to a schedule or a routine, and the use of proper sanitary procedures are more important than fancy equipment for proper monitoring.

Summary

Membranes have been successfully employed to give both

ultimate clarity and stability since the late 1960s. With proper design, attention to sanitation and routine integrity testing and monitoring, this technology can be easily managed.

Before buying expensive housings, filter media and monitoring equipment, it is best to consult with reputable suppliers of both membrane filters and monitoring equipment. Their experience can help you establish both economical and proven performance in aseptic filling.

Peter M. Meier, who wrote this presentation with John Hoechlin, has been employed by Millipore Corp. in Bedford, Mass., for thirteen years in research and development, applications engineering and marketing and sales. He is currently the North American marketing manager for Process Food and Beverage Filtration. He is a member of Master Brewers Association of the America's District New York and the American Society of Enology and Viticulture.

Chapter 17.

BIOREMEDIATION: NATURE'S WAY OF TREATING WASTEWATER

*Sean Duddy,
Polybac Corporation*

If they haven't already begun to do so, brewers and beverage producers throughout the United States are going to have to reassess the ways they use and dispose of one of their most critical resources—water. Last year, the Environmental Protection Agency (EPA) established a wide array of new regulations affecting water treatment practices. These regulations call on the private sector to play a part in protecting environmental resources. For violations, they set forth fines and penalties that could bring businesses to a stop.

The new laws regulate the discharge of hazardous wastes into sewage systems leading to Publicly Owned Treatment Works (POTWs). They are intended to safeguard the nation's water quality. Their effect on microbrewers will be to dramatically change water disposal and drainage practices. In some instances, beverage manufacturers will be able to pay a premium rate for the right to continue to use local water treatment services, but this will require high surcharge costs and constantly monitoring released waters. In other instances, beverage manufacturers, including microbrewers, will opt for the cost savings and efficiencies of on-site, closed-loop water treatment systems. My presentation addresses some of the mandatory changes that must occur in microbrewers' treatment of water resources and also the role that inexpensive, biological pollution control systems can play in helping microbrewers make those changes. Low-cost, closed-loop water treatment systems can easily be attached to microbrewing machinery. These bioremediation tools can restore water to safe standards and allow recycled water to be used again on-site.

EPA Rules Compel Businesses to Protect and Preserve Water Resources

The EPA's recent water treatment regulations are in keeping with the Public Safety Standards set by the Resource Conservation and Recovery Act and the 1990 Water Quality Act. As a result of these laws, state and local environmental requirements will now be more consistent, and enforcement will likely become much more aggressive.

The cleanliness called for by the EPA's new water-use-and-treatment standards will not be attained without expense; it will, depending on the pollution-reduction methods chosen, add to unit production costs. But the return on the business community's investment will be cleaner waterways and uncontaminated wells for ourselves today and our children tomorrow.

Very few American manufacturers will be unaffected by these new EPA rules. Most industries will be forced to dramatically change the ways they use, treat and dispose of water. Many will have to tackle these problems at the same time they are also being called upon to meet new air-quality controls. For food processors, including brewers, pollution prevention will soon be—if it is not yet—as important a concern as sanitation and disease control.

A recent "Science Advisory Report" being circulated by the

EPA's Office of Water indicates that "end of pipe controls and waste disposal should be the last line of defense, not the front line. Preventing pollution at the source is usually a far cheaper, more effective way to reduce environmental risk, especially over the long term."

Water that has been used to clean equipment and bottles and carry discarded or spilled beer into drainpipes and municipal sewers will now be subjected to sliding-scale surcharges by POTWs. These sewage-treatment and water-supply services will have no option but to pass on their increased handling costs to the industrial processors that generate potentially harmful and toxic wastes. Microbrewers, as generators of wastewater that could affect aquatic life and sludge, will probably have to pay high premiums to release their spent water into sewage lines.

POTWs' surcharges to microbrewers and other manufacturers will be levied on the basis of the effect that discharged waste beer and detergent-tainted water could have on the water treatment facility's eco-system and cleaning processes. Too much yeast or detergent—though not dangerous on face value—could reduce biological oxygen demand in waterways and result in a fish kill or a breakdown at the treatment facility.

For those processors who discharge spent water into nearby streams, brooks or holding ponds, the costs of discharge permits and delays caused by monitoring and water-quality testing could prove prohibitive. Discharging into open waterways or underground wells could affect local aquifers and expose business operators to fines and, in some cases, criminal penalties. Furthermore, the EPA's Office of Water has enlisted state environmental agencies to adopt pollution prevention approaches outlined in its National Pollution Discharge Elimination System permit program. These will make it increasingly difficult and costly for industries to move process wastewater to off-site treatment facilities.

Minimizing Waste to Reduce Pollution Prevention Costs

It is evident that American businesses are going to have to find ways to hold down waste-management costs by reducing their generation of waste materials. Household waste recycling and municipal waste collection practices have been stressing source reduction as a critically important economy for solid waste management. The same holds true for water resource management at breweries and bottling facilities.

Handling water treatment at the processing site is one way business operators can control costs and production schedules. For microbrewers, this will mean cleaning process waters with tools that can treat and recycle water at their breweries. The technology to do this is available, relatively inexpensive, and adaptable to the constraints of microbrewing equipment and processing practices.

Using Bioremediation to Reclaim Wastewater

Bioremediation is a process that uses microorganisms to transform harmful substances into non-hazardous materials. It relies on the same scientific principles that permit brewers to use yeast to produce beer. In the broadest sense, it uses the life cycle of naturally occurring microbes to bring about desired chemical and physical changes in a confined and controlled environment.

In essence, bioremediation is a technology that is as old as the Earth. It is the process whereby the hydrocarbons that make up the mass of this biosphere are recycled. Wastewater treatment plants use bioremediation to reclaim sewage waters. Composting centers rely on bioremediation to generate new soil from organic materials.

By employing bioremediation technologies, microbrewers can reclaim water used in their production processes and recycle it for brewing and bottling purposes. The practice of clarifying water with a bioremediation filtration tool and circulating it for reuse is the same as the one used at local water treatment facilities. Microorganisms, like all life forms, need nutrients such as nitrogen, phosphate, trace metals, and carbon to survive. In the course of their life cycle, they break down a wide variety of organic (carbon-containing) compounds found in nature to obtain energy for their growth. Among the compounds that microbes can use as a food source are petroleum hydrocarbons, complex hydrocarbon chains found in detergents and waste beers, and contaminants as toxic as PCBs and cleaning solvents. They are not effective in treating metal contaminants, and like all other life forms, they are adversely effected by radiation.

BioMass Engineering practices, patented by Polybac Corporation, use benign groups of microorganisms to eliminate pollutants from contaminated materials. The equipment and materials that this treatment method requires have been designed to harness the role that microbes play in the life cycle. Nontoxic bacteria consume (or biodegrade) pollutants and when an ecological balance is reached, they simply die off or fall back to a level that can be sustained by the treated site or body of water. The biological treatments synthesize wastes into harmless enzymes, new cell matter or gases. Dissolved substances are removed and destroyed or converted to a colloidal material.

This process of bringing together contaminated water and the microbial mixtures can occur in relatively compact filter tanks. These tanks and the plumbing and monitoring attachments that come with them are relatively inexpensive additions to microbrewing systems. They can help microbrewers clarify water efficiently and reuse it for production processes on continual basis.

The costs of running a small, on-site water treatment set-up is a few cents per thousand gallons. When this outlay is compared to the unchecked expense of POTW surcharges and the exposure to publicly mandated fines and penalties, the bioremediation alternative becomes very appealing and practical.

Closed-loop water treatment systems can be retrofit onto microbrewing equipment. The systems vary in size and scale depending on the user's volume and needs. Small systems that use little electrical power and hold several hundred gallons at any moment are available. They require a limited number of supplies including toxic testing seeds that allow anyone who can read and write to test the quality of treated water, microbial mixtures of dry seeded cells that quickly degrade detergents and waste beer, and nutrient chemicals that speed up the process and keep the clarifying agents up to speed.

Bioremediation products are used in oil fields, refineries, municipal water treatment facilities, health care and pharmaceutical industries, paper and pulp factories and at food processing centers around the world. The technology works and works around the clock. It will make your job easier and help you stay in line with new environmental laws. It's our job to help you use nature to make the world a better place.

Sean Duddy, regional sales manager for Polybac Corporation, is an authority on bioremediation as a waste reduction and disposal tool. At Polybac's laboratories in Bethlehem, Pennsylvania, a staff of scientists and technicians can help microbrewers design water treatment systems that meet federal, state and local standards. Although some charges are made for lab testing of water and waste beer samples (if required), this service is made available at no cost when a bid is sought.

Chapter 18.

INDUSTRY UNDER ATTACK

*Jeffrey G. Becker,
The Beer Institute*

What is neoprohibition? Is it something we need to worry about and when is it going to go away? The neoprohibition movement probably started sometime in the late 1970s with a very small group of individuals who, like the Women's Christian Temperance Union, saw very little redeeming social value in the products that you make and people like me enjoy. That small group of people has now grown to encompass parts of the federal government, plus a new growth industry called *advocacy*. There has been tremendous growth in what is called the *alcoholism treatment field*. One person I met at a meeting for the Office of Substance Abuse Prevention told me that our best customers are their best customers. He is a state coordinator of an alcohol and drug abuse agency, and I thought that was an interesting comment from him. It's interesting that there is a growth industry that exists to beat up on alcohol. I have wondered why people berate alcohol, or in our case, beer. One reason is that most people involved in this neoprohibition movement could be considered to be liberal in their mindset; they believe that government control is the best control. They don't believe that people have the right to make decisions

themselves. On the other side are the people who work for the Center for Science in the Public Interest (CSPI) or government agencies such as the National Institute on Alcohol Abuse and Alcoholism or the Office of Substance Abuse Prevention. These are the major players today. First, because they have the loudest voices, and second because they have the most money. Because they are government agencies, they also control the purse strings; the minute you say something good about the industry, you can pretty much kiss your federal funding goodbye.

I want to examine some of the major events that have occurred over the last several years, talk about the strategy behind them and provide you with some insight on what we at the Beer Institute are doing. First, as you know, because you now have to pay for it, you are required to put a warning label on your containers. There's legislation pending in both the House and the Senate that would mandate that labeling for advertising, also. One reason we fought labeling so hard in 1988, is that we were against the stigma attached to placing a label on a product. People on the other side of the issue saw labeling as being absolutely necessary to provide information to the general public. Yet labeling was one of the many steps that was taken very early in the fight to try to make tobacco unacceptable. It is interesting that people are now claiming that the warning label on tobacco ads and the lack of tobacco advertising today is largely responsible for the decrease in consumption. Yet, most people who know anything about demographics and public opinion know that it was the public's attitude about smoking that turned the trend downward, and not just because of a mandated label and a ban on television advertising. Obviously, a key strategy is to try to attack the product.

The disease of alcoholism as a preventable or treatable illness is a concept we have worked very hard to make people aware of. The public health model, which perhaps you probably don't know much about, is important because it is the basis for many of the decisions and policies that neoprohibitionism supports. It involves the host, or agent, which in our case is alcohol, and the environment. Under the heading of controls, you find such activities as manipulating prices through taxation; limiting availability through hours of closure; limiting advertising venues—specifically billboards and hours when it is appropriate to air beer commercials on television or radio; limiting the number of alcohol licenses in a given area; and limiting the number of licenses to operate a brewpub or a brewery. Neoprohibitionists focus mainly on the environment because that is where they feel the most ground can be gained.

As the agent, alcohol itself is interesting. I was at a meeting about two years ago where one of the leading people trotted out a series of slides on control availability theory based on taxing advertising prices. The fellow proposed by by the year 2000, there would only be four types of beer: a very low alcohol beer, a nonalcoholic brew, a light beer, and a dark beer. There would be only one producer and that would be the government. It struck me as being very odd that they had become so sophisticated and brash as to suggest that within less than a decade, they will have turned brewing over to the federal government!

Let's shed some light on who these people are. CSPI was one of the groups that was very active in promoting putting warning labels in our products, and today, it has also put together a coalition of folks who would like to see our advertisements carry a warning label. They have been the leading group, with help from a group called the Advocacy Institute. The Advocacy Institute basically helps people deal with the media, so when you hear the phrase "alcohol, like crack cocaine and heroin," it is stated that way for a reason. Media has been inundated by groups like the federal government's Office for Substance Abuse Prevention—funded with your and my federal tax dollars—that put out information equating alcohol with illicit drugs. Today, there is a saying that if you don't use the proper words, chances are you aren't going to get money from the federal government.

The Advocacy Institute did to tobacco what tobacco is facing right now. CSPI took the challenge and changed the way the media thought about alcohol, the idea being that once you change the way the media talks about something, public opinion follows. Groups have gone to the media with wild stories and factoids. If you don't know what a factoid is, I will explain. Factoids developed during the Reagan administration. President Ronald Reagan once said that one particular tree gave out about ten times as much carbon monoxide as an average automobile. The next day he gave a speech, and there was a big sign on the tree that said, "Please stop me before I kill again."

Two weeks ago I heard a factoid applied to alcohol. I was at a meeting on impaired driving initiative, which was frightening for me because they are advocating 0.04 percent blood alcohol and we were getting used to them talking about 0.8. Someone put up a slide that said, "Do you know that if you equate drunk driving to airline crashes that the number of people killed by drunk drivers is equal to twenty-three "747s" crashing every week?" This is the type of information that is being couched in factoids that help present a very devastating view of alcohol. I should add that alcohol problems over the last decade have been going down.

Another thrust is one I don't want to call a socialist model, but it certainly is much practiced in Soviet countries, and that is the *control availability theory*. There is the idea that you can legislate morality, that if only one person's life is saved, then we should get beer commercials off the air. To me, that doesn't make a lot of sense. People don't learn to drink from beer commercials, they learn to drink from people like you and me. It is mostly our behavior that we would hope that they would emulate.

Another group that has been very active in this movement is called the National Council on Alcoholism and Drug Dependence. They lobby in Washington spreading half-truths that alcohol is the devil incarnate and that we as brewers, vintners and distillers are out to get their kids and other people addicted to alcohol. Every year people in the movement hold the Alcohol Policy Meetings, and if you would like to develop a little thicker skin, you should go. It is fascinating to have people say to you, "Geez, what does it feel like to be the wolf?" I have never felt like that before. I believe in what we have done to promote educating people about alcohol and dealing with alcohol problems. You cannot raise prices and effectively reduce the consumption of the people least likely to be price-sensitive—alcohol abusers. Taking beer ads off the air is not going to cause them to forget about beer, nor will it stop young people from drinking.

Let me talk about what we at the Beer Institute are doing. We are involved in several programs we believe will be very helpful in getting our word out, and the one I am most proud of is our Beer Institute Community Assistance Fund. It provides grants up to $10,000 for community groups nationwide; thus far, we have given out sixty grants in twenty-eight states. It has been a very successful program. We are trying to interface with people at the community level because that is where the action is. Alcohol education is a ground-up kind of thing.

Another one of our programs is our Safe Holiday Reminder Series. We provide public service announcements to over 1,000 radio stations six times a year encouraging people not to drive drunk or ride with a drunk driver. We have been able to get some sports celebrities involved, and it has been a very nice program that has gotten the message out. As an aside, of the number of responsible drinking and antidrunk driving commercials on the air today, somewhere between 75 and 80 percent are sponsored by beer companies. Gary Heurich (Olde Heurich Brewing Company in Washington, D.C.) always ends his radio ads by saying, "Please drink these products responsibly." So each of us can do something to promote the idea that ours is a responsible industry. If you need information, we have a wealth of information on very creative programs that work. We encourage each of you to work in your local communities. If you know of programs in your local communities that are in need of a little money, let us know. Truly, we can make a difference.

It is important to know that we have made a lot of progress against this movement. We have begun a regular series of meetings with people at the Department of Health and Human Services and with people within the administration. We have been working very closely with the National Highway Traffic Safety Administration on their "buckle up campaign," and we will be pursuing other programs with them to deal with repeat offenders—people who drive on revoked and suspended licenses.

Over the last few weeks I have been to several meeting with the Office of Substance Abuse Prevention. It is disconcerting on one hand because there are tax dollars being used against us and we haven't even being invited to attend the meetings, but now we have finally fought our way back into the process. For the first time in a decade, we will have at least one person involved in a planning conference for the Health and Human Services secretary's meeting coming up this spring to discuss alcohol. So, there are a few bright spots.

At this time, there are three documents of serious interest to us. One is from the National Commission on Drug-Free Schools, which put out a report attacking us on two fronts: advertising and taxation. It is based on the control availability theory. Another is "Healthy People 2000," which sets public health goals for the nation on a variety of topics—alcohol being one—to be accomplished by the year 2000. It proposes a lot of legislative, law enforcement, crack-down approaches that seem an anathema to the way a free democratic society works. The third document is the "Surgeon General's Workshop Report of 1988," a conference where representives of the prohibition movement were invited, but we weren't. It has been sort of a benchmark for a lot of little state groups. Those are the three major federal government documents that do concern me a bit because the presumption is that government policy has moved away from the idea that the marketplace is a better control than the government. It seems that government is looking more at control than at anything else.

Jeffrey G. Becker is vice president at the Beer Institute in the Office of Alcohol Issues, where he addresses various aspects of alcohol issues such as responsible consumption and anti-drunk driving. He was formerly with the National Licensed Beverage Association.

Chapter 19.

CURRENT BREWING ISSUES

*W. Andrew Patton,
Small Brewers Coalition*

There are a number of organizations in the brewing industry, among them the Brewers Association of America—traditionally a trade organization for small brewers, the Beer Institute—a national trade organization sponsored primarily by senior members of the brewing industry, and the Small Brewers Coalition—organized by some senior members of the small brewing industry. Back in the early 1980s, thirteen small brewers got together after hearing about a proposal to increase the federal excise tax on beer. At that time, there was a differential of two dollars per barrel between taxes paid on the first 60,000 barrels brewed and that over 60,000 barrels, and they wanted to preserve that differential.

The microbrewing and brewpub industry has grown up since then and certainly indicates that the U.S. brewing industry is open to entry by entrepreneurs and is alive and well but on a different scale and in a different situation than the big breweries. Now, basically every small brewer pays substantially less excise tax than he or she would if the Small Brewers Coalition, in conjunction with the Beer Institute, the Institute for Brewing Studies, individuals in the brewing industry, and some microbrewers had not been very

active during the past seven years. Today, there are seven senior members remaining from those original thirteen, so you can see that the industry has changed. Today, the Small Brewers Coalition has about sixty members—seven of which are small brewers and the rest microbrewers and pub-brewers. Many of them are here at this Conference today.

Over the past year, we have published several memoranda on issues of the General Agreement on Tariff's and Trade (GATT). Many of you have received our analyses and appraisals of the GATT challenge. Addressing these issues is much broader than the Coalition's original focus, which was only the federal excise tax. But with the activities of the Brewers Association of Canada our mission has broadened.

The complaint of the Canadian brewers regards primarily federal excise tax differentials and certain state tax exemptions. Basically, the Canadians don't want the small brewer to have those benefits. The excise tax differentials date back to the 1950s, although it was in 1989, that the differential for the small brewer (under 2 million barrels) rose to $11 per barrel on the first 60,000 barrels brewed while those who produce over that amount pay $18 per barrel. This differential was maintained so that small brewers and brewpubs do not have to pay the amount of tax that our bigger brothers do on a portion of their production. It certainly doesn't mean new money in any brewer's pocket.

The Brewers Association of Canada has provoked this GATT complaint as a reaction to perceived advantages of beers produced in the U.S. However, the excise tax credit is based on annual production. The GATT requires that domestic products receive no less favorable treatment than import products. The tax benefits that flow to the small brewers are seen by the Canadians as more favorable treatment, either directly or indirectly.

These issues are the present primary focus of the Small Brewers Coalition. We have gathered information from you and other sources, analyzed it, and supplied the attorneys for the U.S. Trade Representative with our analyses and information. On its face, a tax differential is a red flag in a GATT challenge, but there are GATT decisions that have been made that could result in a favorable outcome. In early 1992, a panel made up of representatives of certain countries will determine whether or not these are a GATT violation. Once that decision has been handed down, they will make a recommendation to the general contracting parties, that is, all of the Council of countries that are parties to GATT. There will be time for negotiation between the parties.

At the Small Brewers Coalition, we are requesting that each of you contact your senators or congresspersons to sensitize them to this issue and urge them to indicate their interest to the Trade Representative. Then, if a negative decision were to be handed down, the Trade Representative would be aware of your representative's political interest during the period of negotiation. If a resolution can't be worked out that would be acceptable to both governments, then the GATT Council—the contracting parties— may either authorize or fail to authorize a retaliation in trade. Any retaliation wouldn't necessarily be against alcoholic products going into Canada; it could be on soap, toothpaste, steel, any product subject to GATT regulations. The theory is that the offending industry might then receive pressure enough from the retaliated-against industries to bring its laws into compliance with the GATT.

One of our tactics has been to demonstrate to the Trade Representative how small an impact in terms of international trade, the small brewer, microbrewer and brewpub actually represents. While our production is very important to each of us and our senior members, in the big picture, we are talking about it being 0.005 percent of the beer market in this country. We're talking about $11 million in tax benefits on a federal level, calculated on 1990

Pre-Conference Tour participant looks over the first full-mash Continental Brewing system at the Rotterdam brewpub in Toronto.

production levels. When you get down to the state tax credit incentives, the numbers become even smaller. Our third focus of defense is to lay the groundwork so that the contracting partners on the GATT issue will not authorize retaliation against the small brewers' excise and state tax. That is our three-pronged plan: first to defeat the GATT challenge; second to make sure our interests are represented in any negotiations undertaken; and third, if we get down to the final level and it all goes against us, to ensure that no retaliation occurs.

As for various state practices, the GATT challenge may be an exercise in futility for the Canadian government. The sale and production of alcohol in the U.S. is controlled by every state and is subject to the 21st Amendment to the Constitution of the United States. That has been pointed out to the U.S. Trade Representative attorneys, and they seem to feel that how the 21st Amendment dovetails into this issue probably would be reflected in the enforcement procedure, if any, after the GATT decision.

I hope I have been able to raise your interest in the Canadian GATT challenge and some of its issues. These issues could affect everyone's bottom line.

W. Andrew Patton represents the Small Brewers Coalition in its government relations efforts. He has been a partner in the Kohnen, Patton and Hunt law firm in Cincinnati, Ohio, since 1974. He earned his law degree from the University of Cincinnati College of Law in 1968.

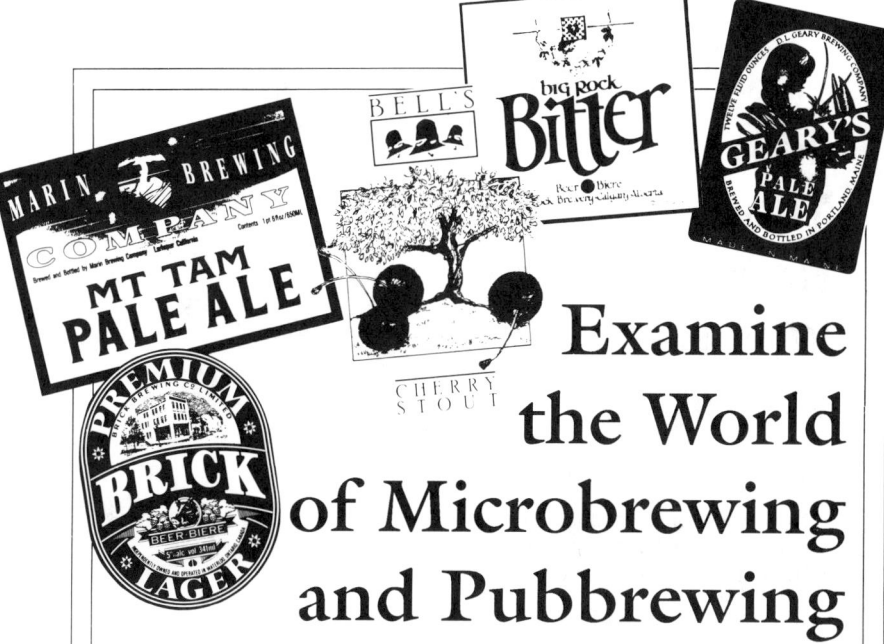

Examine the World of Microbrewing and Pubbrewing

Travel the world of commercial, small-scale brewing; the realm of microbrewers and pubbrewers.

The New Brewer magazine guides you through this new industry. Its pages introduce you to marketing, finance, operations, equipment, recipes, interviews—in short, the whole landscape.

Subscribe to *The New Brewer* and become a seasoned traveler.

NO RISK OFFER

Subscribe now and receive six issues.
If you're not completely satisfied, we'll refund you completely.

$55 a year (U.S.) $65 (Foreign)

Published by The Institute for Brewing Studies, PO Box 1510, Boulder, CO 80306-1510, (303) 447-0816

The New Brewer
THE MAGAZINE FOR MICRO AND PUB-BREWERS

THE AMERICAN HOMEBREWERS ASSOCIATION'S
MAGAZINE FOR HOMEBREWERS AND BEER LOVERS

Join the Thousands of Homebrewers Who Read *zymurgy*

Learn What's New in Homebrewing Including:

- New Recipes • Product Reviews • Tips for Beginners • Beer News
- New Brewing Techniques • Equipment and Ingredients
- Beer History • And Much, Much More!

SATISFACTION GUARANTEED!

Published five times a year by the American Homebrewers Association, *zymurgy* is included with membership.

Mail This Coupon Today! Or call now for credit card order at (303) 447-0816, FAX (303) 447-2825.

_____ ENCLOSED IS $25 FOR ONE FULL YEAR
(CANADIAN/FOREIGN MEMBERSHIPS ARE $30 US)
_____ PLEASE CHARGE MY CREDIT CARD ☐ VISA ☐ MC

CARD NO. _____ EXP. DATE _____

SIGNATURE _____

NAME _____

ADDRESS _____

CITY _____ STATE/PROVINCE _____

ZIP/POSTAL CODE _____ COUNTRY _____

PHONE _____

Make check to: American Homebrewers Association, PO Box 1510, Boulder, CO 80306 USA

Books for your Brewing Library...
from Brewers Publications

All prices are quoted in U.S. dollars. Prices may change and shipping charges vary. For information, write or call: Association of Brewers, PO Box 1679, Boulder, CO 80306-1679 USA. Telephone (303) 447-0816, FAX (303) 447-2825.

Dictionary of Beer and Brewing
This valuable reference will make an outstanding contribution to any brewing library! Author Carl Forget has compiled 1,929 essential definitions used in beermaking, including: Brewing Processes • Ingredients • Types and Styles of Beer • Abbreviations • Arcane Terms • Also: Conversion Tables for temperatures, alcohol percentages and factors.
6 x 9, 180 pp. **Suggested retail price $19.95**

Brewing Lager Beer
This classic reference book is a must for serious brewers interested in all-grain brewing and recipes. First, author Greg Noonan describes the brewing process and ingredients in plain English. Then he guides you through planning and brewing seven classic lager beers—including recipes. As a bonus, the tables of brewing information are excellent.
5 1/2 x 8 1/2, 313 pp. 4th Printing. **Suggested retail price $14.95**

Brewing Mead
Mead is a wonderful honey wine with great, untapped commercial value. Charlie Papazian gives step-by-step recipes and instructions for making several varieties of this honey-based brew. Mead was the beverage of royalty in Europe and was reportedly a powerful aphrodisiac. Lt. Col. Robert Gayre of Scotland gives its history. Now is the time to discover the exotic secrets of mead.
5 1/2 x 8 1/2, 200 pp. 2nd Printing. **Suggested retail price $11.95**

Best of Beer and Brewing
From the transcripts of the 1982-1985 Conferences on Beer and Brewing
Rather than reprint all four transcripts, we chose the very best 15 talks from the four Conferences, asked the authors to update them, and compiled them in one valuable, affordable volume.
5 1/2 x 8 1/2, 260 pp. **Suggested retail price $17.95**

Beer and Brewing, Vol. 7
Transcript of the 1987 Conference on Quality Beer and Brewing
This collection gives readers the widest range of beer information ever published in a single volume. Suited for commercial and homebrewers. Its 17 chapters include: Yeast Strain Traits • Recipe Formulation • Brewing to Scale • Brewing in Your Environs • Origin of Beer Flavor • Innovations in Equipment • Beer Folklore • Contemporary Brewing • Plus ten more.
5 1/2 x 8 1/2, 280 pp. **Suggested retail price $20.95**

Beer and Brewing, Vol. 8
Transcript of the 1988 Conference on Quality Beer and Brewing

There's a world of beer in this transcript, from practical brewing techniques to a perspective of beers abroad given by European brewers. Chapters include: Improved Record-Keeping • Practical All-Grain Brewing • Aroma ID Kit Development • Making Amazing Mead • Brewpubs in Austria.

5 1/2 x 8 1/2, 220 pp.   Suggested retail price $20.95

Beer and Brewing, Vol. 9
Transcript of the 1989 Conference on Quality Beer and Brewing

Here are the transcripts from the biggest AHA Conference ever. This exciting book recaptures the spirit of the event and overflows with invaluable tips in each of its 13 chapters, including: What Makes an Ale an Ale • Clear Beer Please! • Hop Madness • Applying Science to the Art of Brewing.

5 1/2 x 8 1/2, 247 pp.   Suggested retail price $20.95

Beer and Brewing, Vol. 10
Transcript of the 1990 Conference on Quality Beer and Brewing

Read all the talks that made four days in Oakland the ultimate homebrew experience. A dozen talks all focused on the quality of beer and beermaking. Chapters include: Beer Blending ala Judy • Slings of Outrageous Fortune • The World of Malt • Carbonating Your Brew • Home Laboratory Culturing.

5 1/2 x 8 1/2, 198 pp.   Suggested retail price $20.95

Brew Free or Die! Beer and Brewing, Vol. 11
Transcript of the 1991 Conference on Quality Beer and Brewing

Brew Free or Die! Beer and Brewing, Vol. 11 gives the homebrewer a wealth of knowledge about brewing, from techniques to recipes, gadgets, computerization and much more. Find out what the experts shared at the 1991 AHA Homebrew Conference in this readable collection of papers. Terry Foster explores pale ale, Greg Noonan counsels on brewing water, Candy Schermerhorn shares her secrets for cooking with beer, and an additional host of experts give their hard-won knowledge in this informative book.

5 1/2 x 8 1/2, 239 pp.   Suggested retail price $20.95

Brewery Operations, Vol. 3
1986 Microbrewers Conference Transcript

The Brewery Operations series books provide practical, tried-and-true suggestions for small-scale brewing and marketing. Chapters include: Wort Production • Marketing the Pubbrewery • Contract Brewing • Yeast and Fermentation • Brewery Public Relations • Cottage Brewing.

5 1/2 x 8 1/2, 180 pp.   Suggested retail price $25.95

Brewery Operations, Vol. 4
1987 Microbrewers Conference Transcript
  Expert information on brewing, marketing, engineering and management. Chapters include: Malt Extract in Microbrewing • Techniques of Major Breweries • Engineering for the Microbrewer • Developing a Marketing Plan • How to Hire Good People • Equipment Systems for the Brewpub • BATF Regulations.
  5 1/2 x 8 1/2, 210 pp.   Suggested retail price $25.95

Brewery Operations, Vol. 5
1988 Microbrewers Conference Transcript
  Are you a brewpub operator, just getting into the industry or thinking of expanding? Then you'll want to know every fact in Brewery Operations, Vol. 5. There were 21 specialized presentations (27 speakers in all) at the 1988 Conference, providing practical information for all brewers. Topics include: Brewery Feasibility Studies • Equipment Design Considerations • Franchising •Working with Distributors • Yeast Handling • Product Development • Expanding Your Brewery.
  5 1/2 x 8 1/2, 330 pp.   Suggested retail price $25.95

Brewery Operations, Vol. 6
1989 Microbrewers Conference Transcript
  Your guide to the rapidly changing environment of pub- and microbreweries. Chapters include: Legislative Initiatives • Handling Regulatory Authorities • Beer Packaging Design • Working with Distributors • Quality Assurance Systems • Current Federal Regulations • Offering Other's Beers.
  5 1/2 x 8 1/2, 205 pp.   Suggested retail price $25.95

Brewery Operations, Vol. 7
1990 Microbrewers Conference Transcript
  Brewery Operations, Vol. 7, the transcripts of the Denver Conference for microbrewers and pubbrewers, reviews the world of the new commercial brewer. Subjects in the published transcripts include Jeff Mendel's industry overview; Charlie Papazian's presentation on off-flavors; Fred Scheer, of Frankenmuth Brewery, on bottling; Dan Gordon, of Gordon Biersch Brewpub, on trub; Joe Risi, of Christopher Joseph Brewery, on operating multiple units, Al Geitner, of Pub Brewing Co., on alternative beverages for the brewpub; John Foley, of Connecticut Brewing Co., on strategic plan for contract brewers and Dan Carey, of J.V. Northwest, on microbrewery design performance.
  5 1/2 x 8 1/2, 212 pp.   Suggested retail price $25.95

Brewing Under Adversity
Brewery Operations, Vol. 8
1991 Microbrewers Conference Transcripts

It is more difficult than ever to run a successful brewing business in today's climate of anti-alcohol sentiment and restrictive legislation. The 1991 Microbrewers Conference, titled "Brewing Under Adversity," addressed this topic and many others pertaining to the smaller brewing venture, and Brewing Under Adversity, Brewery Operations, Vol. 8, brings this information to you. Topics include: Brewing Under Adversity, Industry Overview, Packaging for the Environment, Brewpub Design Efficiency and Operating Multiple Units.

5 1/2 x 8 1/2, approx. 240 pp.   Suggested retail price $25.95

Brewers Resource Directory

Here are the updated phone numbers, addresses, personnel and descriptions of North American breweries and suppliers you've been waiting for! We know how valuable this publication is by the thousands sold to date. It's the most definitive directory in the industry. You get complete listings for: Microbreweries and Brewpubs • Ingredient Suppliers • Brewing Consultants • Equipment Manufacturers • Large Breweries • Associations and Publications • State Laws and Excise Taxes. Updated and published yearly.

Plus, an informative article and statistics summarizing the year's activities and trends.

8 1/2 x 11, 281 pp.   Suggested retail price $80.00

Brewery Planner
A Guide to Opening Your Own Small Brewery

When planning to open a brewery, it only makes sense to find out everything you can from those who have already learned about the business, sometimes the hard way. Brewery Planner is designed to prepare the new brewer for every potential obstacle or necessity. It is a collection of articles written by experienced brewers, covering The Physical Plant in Section One, Tips from the Experts in Section Two, Marketing and Distribution in Section Three, and Business Plan, Including Templates for Financial Statements in Section Four. A must for anyone planning to open a brewery.

8 1/2 x 11, 191 pp.   Suggested retail price $80.00

The New Brewer

The New Brewer magazine is designed to address the needs of the serious, small-scale commercial brewer. We provide up-to-date facts about: Technical Data on Brewing • Reports on Brewing Equipment • Marketing Strategies • Beer Styles Worldwide • Current Industry News • Legal and Tax Issues • Public Relations • New Product Reviews • Profiles of Breweries • Employee Management • Brewery Safety.

50 pages per issue. Published six times yearly.
$55/Year (U.S.) $65/Year (Foreign)

The Winners Circle
There is no other book like it! 126 award-winning homebrew recipes for 21 styles of lager, ale, and mead.
Start brewing with this refreshing collection of tried-and-true homebrew recipes selected from the winners of the AHA National Homebrew Competition.
5 1/2 x 8 1/2, 196 pp.   Suggested retail price $11.95

Principles of Brewing Science
George Fix has created a masterful look at the chemistry and biochemistry of brewing. With a helpful short course in the appendix, this book will unravel the mysteries of brewing, showing you what really goes on during the making of beer and how you can improve it. An absolute must for those who want to get the most out of their brewing.
5 1/2 x 8 1/2, 250 pp.   Suggested retail price $29.95

Pale Ale
First in the Classic Beer Style Series

Terry Foster, a British expatriate and renowned expert on British beers has created a technical masterpiece on pale ale, the world's most popular style of ale. Written with an entertaining historical perspective, this book more than measures up to its subject matter.

Chapters include history, character, flavor, ingredients, brewing, methods and comparisons of commercial pale ales.
5 1/2 x 8 1/2, 140 pp.   Suggested retail price $11.95

Continental Pilsener
Second in the Classic Beer Style Series

Learn the ingredients and techniques that produce this golden, distinctively hopped lager. Dave Miller, an award-winning brewer and author, takes you through the history, flavor, ingredients and methods of the beer that revolutionized brewing.

You'll also learn about current commercial examples of the style. Professionals and homebrewers alike will enjoy this exploration of a classic beer.
5 1/2 x 8 1/2, 102 pp.   Suggested retail price $11.95

Lambic
Third in the Classic Beer Style Series

Lambic, by Jean-Xavier Guinard, is the only book ever published that completely examines this exotic and elusive style. From origins to brewing techniques, Lambic unravels the mysteries that make this rare style so popular. Lambic contains the only directory of the lambic breweries of Belgium. Guinard, a student of Dr. Michael Lewis at the University of California at Davis, grew up in the shadow of lambic breweries and combined vocation and avocation to produce this wonderful book.
5 1/2 x 8 1/2, 169 pp.   Suggested retail price $11.95

Vienna
Fourth in the Classic Beer Style Series

Vienna, a dark, delicious lager, has never been easier to brew. George Fix, well known homebrewer and beer scientist, and his wife, Laurie, explore the history and techniques of this style, giving recipes and in-depth instructions.

Brewers have long known that this is a difficult beer to make true to style—but Vienna, the first book to explore this lager, helps even beginning brewers master it.

5 1/2 x 8/12, approx. 160 pp.   **Suggested retail price $11.95**

Porter
Fifth in the Classic Beer Style Series

In the mid-eighteenth century, porter was such a popular beer style that some of the fermenting vats were large enough for 100-200 people to dine in them during their inauguration. But more recently, this style was almost lost to modern beerlovers. Today porter is making a comeback, and Terry Foster brings to homebrewers the history, techniques and lore of this rich brew. Porter is the only book available on the style, and it is one of the most colorfully written and enjoyable beer style books available.

5 1/2 x 8 1/2, approx. 170 pp.   **Suggested retail price $11.95**